D0875570

Manners in the Netherlands

The Dutch Ditz

Also written by Reinildis van Ditzhuyzen and available in Dutch as part of this series:

❖   *Hoe hoort het eigenlijk? De Dikke Ditz* (On your best behaviour? The Complete Ditz),
    fully revised edition 1999, 36th printing: 2009.

❖   *De Dunne Ditz. Hoe hoort het eigenlijk?* (The Handy Ditz. On your best behaviour?),
    2008, 2nd printing: 2009.

❖   *De KinderDitz. Kinderen weten hoe het hoort* (The Kid's Ditz. Children know best!),
    2008, 3rd printing: 2009.

REINILDIS VAN DITZHUYZEN

MANNERS
IN
THE NETHERLANDS

The Dutch Ditz

BECHT — HAARLEM

© 2009 Reinildis van Ditzhuyzen, The Hague

© 2009 Uitgeverij J.H. Gottmer / H.J.W. Becht BV

PO Box 317, 2000 AH Haarlem, The Netherlands

(e-mail: post@gottmer.nl)

Uitgeverij J.H. Gottmer / H.J.W. Becht BV is part of the Gottmer Publishing Group

© 2009 English translation: Lorraine T. Miller - Epicycles, Amsterdam

Illustrations: Atelier van Wageningen, Amsterdam

Cover and book design: Mark van Wageningen, Amsterdam

Printing and binding: Wilco, Amersfoort

ISBN 978 90 230 1259 7 / NUR 451

Table of Contents

Throughout the book the reader can find various academic propositions, mostly typical of the Dutch mentality.

Introduction:

Why this book?

NEDERLAND – EXPAT-LAND

Nederland or the Netherlands is a small country where a relatively large number of expats (temporarily) live. Incidentally, the word expat is a fairly modern term. It's an abbreviation of the word expatriate and is defined as 'a person living in a country that is not his or her own'. However, this term does not apply to all immigrants. Expats tend to include only those who find themselves abroad for a longer period of time, particularly the employees of internationally operating organisations who have been posted abroad. In the Netherlands, this pertains to the employees of more than thirty international organisations, for instance, the European Patent Office, Europol, the International Court of Justice (ICJ), the International Criminal Tribunal for the former Yugoslavia (ICTY), the Organisation for the Prohibition of Chemical Weapons (OPCW), as well as the employees of multinational companies such as Shell and Unilever, in addition to a myriad of diplomats. Expats such as these move home regularly, trekking like modern-day nomads from country to country. This term often denotes a rather privileged, financially secure group of people with tax-free incomes.

However, there are also other sorts of expats, for instance, the so-called independents or free movers. As national barriers to em-

ployment give way due to an expanding European Union, people have become more and more flexible. They move from country to country to work for the employer of their choice and to secure the job they desire. This is a large and growing group.

Finally, the international community in the Netherlands also includes so-called knowledge (im)migrants, a growing number of foreign students and migrants from Eastern Europe (skilled crafts-men).

All these people have a single thing in common: the time they will spend living in the Netherlands is open-ended. Many of them may only be here for a few years; others could be here the rest of their lives. Then again, they might be living in another country next year.

❖❖❖

Holland and the Netherlands

In this book, the name *Nederland* (the Netherlands) – not Hol-land – is used to refer to this country. In the same way that England is a part of Great Britain, Holland is a part of the Neth-erlands. Present-day Holland is comprised of two provinces of the Netherlands: North Holland (capital city Haarlem) and South Holland (capital city Den Haag = The Hague in English). In addition to this, there are ten other provinces including Flevoland, Gelderland, Zeeland and Limburg. The province of Friesland even has its own official language. Just keep this in mind: every *Hollander* (Dutch person from Holland) is a *Neder-*

lander (from the Netherlands), but not every *Nederlander* is a *Hollander*. And the capital of the Netherlands is not Den Haag (The Hague), which people often think, but Amsterdam. The Hague is both the residence of the head of state (Queen Beatrix) and the government seat, and is also therefore home to many foreign diplomats.

❖❖❖

Uncertainty about practices and customs

Every expatriate, upon arriving in a new country, comes up against practices and customs that are unfamiliar or that he or she might not understand. This can cause a person to feel insecure about how they should best behave or react. In the Netherlands, an expat might wonder:
 – What is the acceptable way of greeting people?
 – When and for whom do you bring along a present? Should it be large or small?
  Sometimes this feeling of uncertainty can make everyday life and work unnecessarily complicated. Moreover, an expat could feel offended because, at a certain moment, a Dutch person does something that is unacceptable according to that expat's cultural perceptions. For instance, when Dutch men are having a meeting they like the atmosphere to be informal. They might lean back and rest a foot on their knee. But displaying the sole of your shoe is

perceived by people from the Middle East as very impolite and even offensive. Think of the angry Iraqi journalist who hurled his shoes at President Bush to show deep contempt!

What is more, the way the Dutch dress often leads to raised eyebrows among expats. A good illustration: a group of Africans came to a conference being held at the Royal Tropical Institute in stylish suits, while their Dutch colleagues appeared in sweaters and tieless shirts. The Africans felt as if they were not being taken seriously.

Therefore, unfamiliarity with the ways of the Dutch can lead to uncertainty and disbelief on the part of foreigners. So it is not inconceivable that they might react inappropriately – and there you have it: a misunderstanding is born. Such a misunderstanding might be amusing and without consequences, but could also lead to considerable trouble.

I once experienced such a mix-up myself. A long time ago in Seville (Spain), I was invited to a friend's home at 10 p.m. Being the Dutch person I am, I ate beforehand – well, that was certainly a mistake. A lavish dinner was waiting including *perdices* (partridges); the proud host had shot them himself. The hospitable family kept encouraging me to dig in. Given my earlier dining experience at home, I simply could not swallow another bite. Nevertheless, to be polite, I shovelled my face full with partridge and the like. Oh, did I feel sick! After dinner, I thought I was going to burst. There was only one solution: digesting all that food as quickly as possible. So to get my digestive juices flowing, escorted by the son of the family,

I trudged off on a walk through the city that felt like it would never end. Since that day, I have not been able to look at partridge, let alone eat any...

As a foreigner, you are somehow always an outsider. This also struck me when I was studying in Vienna, because I was continually characterised by my Austrian friends as *die komische Holländerin* (that funny Dutch girl).

ASSUMPTIONS ABOUT EXPATS

The Dutch are not bashful about telling you what they think about foreigners that live here. Some perceive them with irritation or even resentment. They are seen as self-centred users, who don't integrate into Dutch society but prefer to inhabit their 'expat bubble' with their own clubs, schools, etc. Some of the assumptions you often hear include that they are rich, live in lavish homes in wealthy villages such as Wassenaar or Aerdenhout, drive flashy cars, send their children to private schools, enjoy extended holidays – and the list continues. And if that isn't enough criticism, they are coddled by their companies and the cities where they live with expat desks.

But this so-called champagne lifestyle is a generalisation. Many Dutch people have little understanding of the complications, the bureaucracy, the stress involved with relocating: living out of suitcases in a hotel, grappling with a strange language, unfamiliar customs, different opening times for shops and businesses, questions such as to queue or not to queue, where do you buy a bus ticket and how do you officially register as a resident with the municipality where you are going to live? Sometimes it's very difficult for expats to find their footing in the Dutch landscape.

To help alleviate problems adjusting to life here and to make the lives of expatriates in the Netherlands easier and more successful, this book deals with the most important conventions of Dutch society. In seven short chapters laced with questions, infoboxes and background information, *The Dutch Ditz* also looks at idiosyncratic behaviour of the Dutch – habits and customs that are different from anywhere else.

✧✧✧

What's up with the Dutch?

Here you will find some English expressions in which the Dutch have played a contributing role. Most are less than flattering... hmm, implying something about English or Dutch speaking people?

- ✧ **Going Dutch** = each person pays his or her own bill in a restaurant.
- ✧ **A Dutch party** = a party to which each guest brings something to eat or drink.
- ✧ **A Dutch auction** = a type of auction where the auctioneer begins with a high asking price which is lowered until a

buyer is willing to accept the auctioneer's price.

- ❖ **I'm a Dutchman if...** = a way of denying a supposition. 'If you are right, then I am a Dutchman' means: I'm absolutely sure you're wrong.
- ❖ **Double Dutch** = nonsense, meaningless words (*Triple Dutch* = even more incomprehensible).
- ❖ **Dutch courage** = false courage obtained by drinking alcohol.
- ❖ **A Dutch wife** = an open frame construction made of cane, originally used in the Dutch East Indies and other hot countries for resting one's limbs; in Japan, a plastic sex doll.
- ❖ **Dutch comfort** = cold comfort, i.e. things could have been worse.
- ❖ **Dutch act** = suicide.
- ❖ **To talk to someone like a Dutch uncle** = to lecture with excessive seriousness.
- ❖ **Dutch gold** = tinsel or imitation gold leaf.
- ❖ **A Dutch headache** = a hangover.

❖❖❖

'To be successfully adapted to the Netherlands, one should have a precise watch, a busy agenda and be constantly complaining about the weather.'
(Isabella A. Nougalli Tonaco, Wageningen University, 2008)

Author's approach

Besides consulting numerous publications while I was writing this book, I made it my business to speak extensively to lots of expatriates, asking them what strikes them personally about the habits, customs and practices of the Dutch: What do they think the Dutch do differently, what do they appreciate, what annoys them, etc.? The expats I consulted come from all different nationalities. They are self-employed or work for companies ranging from large to small, embassies, international institutions and organisations. Furthermore, to have an overview that would be as broad and reliable as possible, I visited so-called expat centres set up by companies and municipalities and spoke to members or heads of expat societies and international clubs.

The wealth of observations and experiences these foreigners shared with me made it surprisingly clear just how 'different' we Dutch actually are – not only different from others, but especially different from how we see ourselves. Consequently, to my pleasant surprise, this book serves yet another purpose: it compels the Dutch to take a good look in the mirror.

So, to my international and Dutch readers alike, lots of success and enjoy *The Dutch Ditz*!

— I —

LIFE IN DUTCH-LAND:

OBSERVATIONS OF EXPATRIATES

Foreigners who move to the Netherlands indicate that they are, for the most part, satisfied with the quality of life here. When asked what they appreciate most about the Netherlands, you often hear the following responses:

- The country has a high standard of living.
- The country has a good road network (apart from frequent traffic jams) plus convenient land, sea and air connections.
- The public transport is good.
- The everyday use of the bicycle (and separate bicycle lanes) is highly attractive.
- Many international businesses have their headquarters here, ensuring opportunities for foreigners.
- English is widely spoken.
- Everything is functioning here! Street lighting, water, electricity, telephone, the entire essential infrastructure related to everyday life is well-organised.
- The Amsterdam area is a leading European business location.
- The educational system is rated as excellent.
- There is a lot to do, particularly for children.
- The landscape is stunning: beautiful cities and villages, dunes, dikes, polders and canals, the sea and beaches, lakes, the different Dutch islands.

❖ Skating on inland waterways, canals and lakes.
❖ The high level of culture here, including diverse museums; all kinds of festivals; ballet; literature; music: Amsterdam's *Koninklijk Concertgebouworkest* was recently chosen as the best in the world, ahead of even the Berliner Philharmoniker and the Wiener Philharmoniker.

And lastly, the personal impressions of four expats about the Dutch:
❖ 'Dutch people are generally open and helpful, and debate and discussion are the order of the day. Most people you meet here are welcoming and friendly to foreigners.'
❖ 'I love the work ethic: "work to live, not live to work".'
❖ 'Five words to describe the Dutch: open-minded, liberal, frugal, environmentally and socially conscious and good business people.'
❖ 'I love that when you smile people always greet you with a *Goedemorgen* (Good morning).'

In short, living here is an attractive though at times challenging experience, but expats are essentially positive about the Netherlands.

❖❖

Dutch Poem of the Century
In 2000, the following poem was chosen by the Dutch as *Gedicht van de Eeuw*, the best poem of the 20th century:

Herinnering aan Holland
Hendrik Marsman (1899–1940)

'Memory of Holland'
(Translation: Paul Vincent)

Denkend aan Holland	Thinking of Holland
zie ik breede rivieren	I see wide-flowing rivers
traag door oneindig	slowly traversing
laagland gaan,	infinite plains,
rijen ondenkbaar	inconceivably
ijle populieren	rarefied poplars
als hooge pluimen	like lofty plumes
aan den einder staan;	on the skyline in lanes;
en in de geweldige	and submerged in the vastness
ruimte verzonken	of unbounded spaces
de boerderijen	the farmhouses
verspreid door het land,	strewn over the land,
boomgroepen, dorpen,	tree clumps, villages,
geknotte torens,	truncated towers,
kerken en olmen,	churches and elm trees –
in een grootsch verband.	all wondrously planned.
De lucht hangt er laag	The sky hangs low
en de zon wordt er langzaam	and slowly the sun by
in grijze veelkleurige	mists of all colours
dampen gesmoord,	is stifled and greyed
en in alle gewesten	and in all the regions
wordt de stem van het water	the voice of the water
met zijn eeuwige rampen	with its endless disasters
gevreesd en gehoord.	is feared and obeyed.

Worth mentioning: the contemporary Dutch writer Thomas Rosenboom, in describing his annoyance with badly-raised Dutch children (also see p. 148), gave the first line of this poem a new interpretation:

Denkend aan Holland	Thinking of Holland
zie ik groepen jongeren	I see groups of loitering youth
breed voor me	boldly blocking the pavement
op de stoepen staan...	in front of me...

❖❖

THE IMPOLITE DUTCH

Without a doubt, there are things in the Netherlands that leave something to be desired. First and foremost being the weather. Many foreigners complain about the awful weather in the Netherlands and experience the piercing Dutch wind and the endless damp as bone chilling. Unfortunately, this aspect of living here is beyond my control.

Besides this, the three most common complaints you hear from expatriates about life in the Netherlands are related to the Dutch health care system ('Doctors have no bedside manners'), the bureaucracy and the level of service (or better said: lack of service). More about this follows directly as well as later in this book.

Dutch health care: All things being equal?

Expats express a lot of dissatisfaction about the health care system in the Netherlands. This is striking, in fact, since comparative studies by the Organisation for Economic Cooperation and Development (OECD) indicate, from a medical-technical point-of-view, that health care in the Netherlands is excellent, equivalent to the care being offered in the United States, North-West Europe, Canada and Australia. To improve the negative image of the Dutch health care system, the Bronovo Hospital in The Hague decided that it was necessary to reach out to expats. Therefore the hospital, which is visited by many expatriates (40,000 of them live in the city), established an expat advisory panel.

The chairman of this committee, lung specialist Dr. Henk Berendsen, shed some light on why expats are dissatisfied: 'There are two underlying reasons: the waiting lists and the way the Dutch deal with patients. To begin with, expats are accustomed to health care systems that are structured differently from here. They also often belong to a privileged part of the population in their own countries, which gives them easy access to good health care. But our system doesn't recognise such a distinction, because well-to-do people do not necessarily come first. So your name might very well end up on a waiting list. Not much can be done about this, but you can certainly explain this more clearly to expats. For that matter, waiting lists only apply to situations that are not considered medically urgent – acute cases always receive immediate attention in the hospitals here.' Berendsen understands that patients usually see their own complaints as urgent, but: 'An egalitarian system has inherent advantages and disadvantages.'

Explaining why some expats feel they are not dealt with considerately enough, Berendsen attributes this in part to the Dutch language: 'Dutch is a kind of seaman's vernacular: to-the-point, rough around the edges, lacking in nuances. It's very different from the English language, which tends to be more polite. It's understandable that foreigners experience the way the Dutch do things as unpleasant at times.'

Meanwhile, specific policies aimed at assisting expats have been put into practice. Berendsen: 'At Bronovo, we are trying to meet expats halfway. It's certainly not our intention to make people who are only going to be here for a short while think like the Dutch, but we are trying to be more hospitable, spend more time explaining the ins & outs of the Dutch system and want to address the fact that foreigners don't always feel welcome here.'

Apart from this initiative, Amsterdam's Academic Medical Center (AMC) is also considering instituting separate services such as these to serve their expat community. (Also consult www.bronovo.nl and www.healthpowerhouse.com).

Last but not least, there is one other complaint you hear a lot from foreigners. It is related to the bad manners of the Dutch. When I asked for a few concrete examples, a torrent of criticism followed.

The Dutch...

- let doors slam closed in your face.
- never say *alsjeblieft, dank je wel* or *sorry* (please, thank you or sorry).
- think they know everything better.
- feel that no matter how horrendously their children behave, it's *leuk* (fun).
- are inclined to be sloppy dressers.
- attract attention to themselves on the Internet and TV/radio by exhibiting vulgarity, banality and over-the-top rowdiness. Insulting cursing matches in chat rooms on the Internet are apparently routine to them, considerably more so than in other countries.

And as far as all this goes, even Dutch people themselves seem to agree with these observations: sixty-one percent of the population considers rudeness to be the number one irritation in society today. It is consequently not surprising that, for some time now, there has been something of an ongoing political discussion about the need for restoring *normen en waarden* (norms and values); that Dutch cities such as Gouda and Rotterdam have introduced their own form of *stadsetiquette* (city manners); or that the current Dutch Prime Minister Balkenende often uses the slogan: *Fatsoen moet je doen,* 'Decency begins with frequency'.

However, this reputation of the Dutch is nothing new under the sun. For centuries, they have been perceived by foreigners as unmannerly and gruff. In the 16th century, the word *crassus* (crass) was the way the Dutch were commonly described. And a century later, the English diplomat and essayist Sir William Temple (1628–1699) called them surly and ill-mannered. The famous French writer Voltaire (1694–1774) only needed three Cs to describe what the Dutch reminded him of: *canaux, canards, canaille* (dikes, ducks, disorderly bunch). By the way, the modern version is: *canaux, canards, cannabis...* The Germans, too, were irritated by the bad manners of the Dutch. The expression *ein echter Holländer* (a true Dutch person) was synonymous with *ein unhöflicher Mensch* (a discourteous human). Leopold Mozart, who visited the Republic of the Netherlands with his son Wolfgang in 1766, characterised the Dutch as *grob* (gruff).

Criticism about the bad manners and rudeness of the Dutch mainly occurred because foreign aristocrats and other VIPs visiting the Netherlands were confronted with a less respectful attitude from the common people than they were used to. In 1781, Emperor Joseph II of Habsburg personally experienced this during his travels through the province of Holland. In the small village of Broek in Waterland, he was interested in taking a closer look inside a Dutch house. At the request of His Majesty's escort asking if the emperor might come inside, the resident responded he would first have to consult with his wife. He returned with the message that his wife was not receiving guests at that moment and shut the door in their faces.

So here you have it. We Dutch are very egalitarian, we don't take kindly to hierarchy.

According to the contemporary British historian Jonathan Israel, this democratic and egalitarian attitude originates primarily from the Eighty Years' War (The Dutch Revolt of 1568–1648), an insurrection against the despotism of monarchs. During and after this revolt, the republic was born – quite unusual and modern for that time. In this republic, the so-called burghers (citizens) ruled the roost – and that was quite unusual too.

The fact that the burghers governed meant aristocrats played a minor role in the country. Grand and noble courts, with refined and elegant manners like in other European countries, were hardly found here. So if there was no exemplary behaviour for these Dutch burghers to emulate, where and how would they learn good manners?

But this didn't seem to matter. Although – or perhaps even because – the Dutch were outspoken and direct, they were highly successful in trade and commerce and made a fortune. This was known as the Dutch Golden Age.

Also important was the French theologian Jean Calvin (Johannes Calvijn, John Calvin, 1509–1564): he exerted a major influence on the Netherlands. Calvin rejected all form of hierarchy and saw nothing in flattery. According to him, one should always acknowledge and accentuate deficiencies in the young and old, the upper-class and lower-class, and never cover up failings with flattery. This is the reason Calvin preferred an austere design for both church and service, so that one did not think receiving God's favour was based on pomp and splendour. This also explains the Dutch preference for frugality. For centuries, moderation and prudence were preached as a virtue for body and soul. American-born James Kennedy, professor of Dutch history at the University of Amsterdam (UvA), points out that the Dutch often consider good manners a form of deception, and courtesy a form of flattery. According to him, the Dutch are still 'cultural Calvinists, both in their matter-of-factness and their thriftiness'.

The emphasis on equality that was encouraged by the Enlightenment in the 18th century still lingers. This attitude of the Dutch is best reflected in thoughts such as: Why should I rise for somebody else? Are they any better than I am? The frequently-heard Dutch expressions *Doe maar gewoon, dan doe je al gek genoeg* (Be normal, then you're crazy enough) and *Niet met je kop boven het maaiveld uitsteken* (Never let your head rise above the parapet) – similar to the English expression: Don't stand out in a crowd – are also good illustrations of this attitude.

In the 1960s and '70s, this mindset only increased in intensity. In those days, there was a strong emphasis on emancipation and assertiveness. Then the slogans were 'Be yourself!' and 'Anything goes!'. An anti-authoritarian approach to raising children was popular, all forms of decorum were nonsense and it was important for people to stand-up for themselves. However, the negative effect of all this was a decrease in respect for others, resulting in an increase in the aforementioned impoliteness.

Etiquette: Typically Dutch?

So, it is a given: the Dutch have traditionally been defined by foreigners as unmannerly and gruff. Nonetheless, it was a Dutchman, Desiderius Erasmus, who in 1530 wrote one of the most popular books ever about good manners and etiquette. His influential booklet was translated into many European languages and reprinted eighty times in the 16th century alone.

Actually, the very French-sounding word *etiquette* is believed to have originated from the Dutch word for label: *etiket*. In the 18th century this word *etiket,* derived from the old-Dutch word *stikken* or *sticken* (to attach), was applied to matters of precedence: people were labelled according to the importance of their rank and position. This word, besides having the meaning of *opstiksel* (label) according to *préséance* (precedence), gradually acquired the meaning of 'rule of precedence', and was later more generally applied to the entire system of behaviour rules.

According to others, however, the notion of etiquette originated in the court of the French King Louis XIV (1638–1715). He had signboards placed beside the lovely sprawling lawns at the Palace in Versailles with the inscription *(étiquette):* 'Do not walk on the grass!'. When people did not adhere to this request, the king issued a decree ordering them 'to obey the inscription' *(s'en tenir à l'étiquette)*. This anecdote could also explain how etiquette acquired its current meaning.

THE DUTCH: STRAIGHTFORWARD OR JUST PLAIN RUDE?

There is one Dutch characteristic that all foreigners seem to agree on: the Dutch are very straightforward; they say what they think. However, not everybody is equally charmed by this trait.

A few direct quotes:

- ❖ **An Irishman:** 'Their directness can sometimes be very hurtful. We Irish have what we call "blarney" – we tend to be more diplomatic.'
- ❖ **A Chinese student in Leiden:** 'A Chinese person would never say that something is stupid. Instead, they would say something "is less suitable". And when they don't want to oblige, they never come out and say this directly. Instead they say: "I would enjoy that, but perhaps some other time".'
- ❖ **A Frenchman:** 'I experience their straightforward manner of approaching people as impolite and pushy. Though you can ask someone a single question without a problem, asking three questions seems to go too far. In France one would simply add an apologetic *si ce n'est pas indiscret* (If you don't mind).'
- ❖ **An American:** 'Expect unwarranted advice or comments on everything ranging from your accent, country of origin, driving abilities and clothing.'
- ❖ **An Englishman:** 'What the Dutch call straightforwardness, I call lack of manners.'
- ❖ **A German:** 'The Dutch have this thing about truth and honesty and they'll tell you the truth even if it rips you up one side and down the other.'

This Dutch straightforwardness is also exemplified by their *bet-weterigheid* (knowing-everything-better syndrome). They immediately have an opinion about everything and, as already mentioned earlier, are not shy about expressing it. A Russian diplomat remembered a story about his first encounter with the Dutch: 'Straight away, they started telling me all about Russia, how things in the country work, what the Russian people are like, etc. I couldn't get a word in edgewise.' And an English expat, who had been playing golf his entire life, told a story about playing a round one afternoon with a Dutch business associate: 'He began explaining the rules to me in minute detail!', the Englishman exclaimed, still somewhat irritated. 'It hadn't crossed his mind that maybe I knew infinitely more about the game of golf than he did... After three holes, I had had enough and I left the green.'

So, it should not astonish anyone that since the 17th century the Dutch have wholeheartedly believed in the expression *De brutalen hebben de halve wereld* (Audacity pays, *Frechheit siegt, La timidité n'a jamais mené au premier rang*). And indeed, with their at times brash way of doing business, the Dutch have not done so badly for themselves.

Schaatsen is een denksport.
'Skating is a mental game.'
(A. ter Elst, Groningen University, 2006)

Culture shock: False expectations

Granted, in some respects the Dutch behave more impolitely than others. But that is only the beginning of the story. Apparently, many expats find living in the Netherlands tantamount to true culture shock. Naturally, anyone who is thrust into unknown surroundings, away from their trusted environment, becomes disoriented. But in the Netherlands foreigners are confronted with a culture gap that they are not expecting. It is primarily that thin layer of similarity compared to their own cultures that catches (western) expats off guard. An Englishman: 'In an Asian or Islamic country you would expect different habits and customs, but not in the Netherlands. Yet, here many things are quite different.'

Add to this the fact that people arrive with false expectations. Before departing, expats are often told: 'The Dutch are so easygoing and tolerant! So informal, too! And don't worry: everybody speaks English.' Well, no wonder you are disappointed, because this is not the reality. Once you are living here, you will quickly realise that the Dutch may seem informal and easygoing, but that they are actually quite formal. A few examples: the importance of shaking hands, punctuality, sticking to a tight schedule and let us not forget that all important coffee break. Contrary to all expectations, the Dutch are fond of strict social rules, which when ignored can lead to problems.

Where does this standing on ceremony come from? Among other things, it is related to the importance the Dutch attach to equality. Some expats assume that it's because the Netherlands is a tiny, over-populated country that is also partially below sea level. To have a good life in this country and for things to function efficiently, everything has been systematically and precisely arranged: dikes, canals, roadways, straight streets with rows of attached houses. Subsequently, the entire country is neat and orderly – similar to its residents.

And as far as their command of English goes: undeniably, many Dutch speak an impressive amount of English and expats are grateful for this. On the other hand, a lot of Dutch people only speak some degree of English but think it's flawless. They not only make mistakes but often translate from Dutch to English in a literal – word-for-word – way. So a phrase that sounds perfectly reasonable and polite in Dutch, could end up sounding extremely condescending and arrogant when it has gone copy-paste to English. Nuances also tend to get lost in translation. Add to this the fact that the Dutch often speak English with the wrong intonation. This can result in foreigners being exposed to statements that are incomprehensible and perhaps unintentionally rude. A Scot provided a pretty good example: 'If I need a pen during a meeting, I would most likely say: "Could you please pass me one of those pens?" While if you translate word-for-word what a Dutch person might say: "*Hé Peter, geef me die pen even!*" you end up with something resembling "Hey Peter, hand me that pen!"' This not only comes across as bossy, but sounds very demanding as well. The same applies to the example below. The Dutch serve coffee and biscuits in a brusque and businesslike way (see left example), which not only sounds unsociable, but is a far cry from how this occurs elsewhere (see right example):

In the Netherlands	Elsewhere
Q: Coffee?	'Can I offer you a cup of coffee?
A: Yes	'Yes, please, thank you!'
Q: Sugar?	'Would you like some sugar?'
A: Two lumps	'Two spoonfuls, please.'
Q: Milk?	'Do you take milk?'
A: No	'No, thank you.'
Q: Biscuit?	'Would you like a biscuit?'
A: Yes	'How nice, yes, please.'

Lastly one more example of the characteristic use of the Dutch language, that might be misunderstood by foreigners. A Dutch woman had to be rushed to a New York City hospital. She was in enormous pain and said to the doctor: 'The pain is driving me crazy; I'm going to climb to the top of the highest building and throw myself off!' The doctor immediately intervened: a psychiatrist was summoned and she was prescribed anti-depressants. He thought that the woman was severely depressed – but she was only expressing herself in a typically Dutch way in English.

And then let's not overlook those literal translations from Dutch to English (also coined as Dunglish) that can often result in embarrassment – phrases such as 'I fock horses' instead of 'I breed horses'; 'Can it or can it not?' instead of 'Do we have a go ahead?'; 'This is wet fingerwork' instead of 'This is rather a sloppy job'; etc. Fortunately the Dutch can also laugh at themselves about this, as the success of a few entertaining books about these at times funny and outrageous errors in translation demonstrates.

If the truth be told, with their straightforwardness the Dutch do not mean anyone any harm. On the contrary, they want to be perceived as forthcoming and friendly. They simply do not realise that all that honesty might have exactly the opposite effect. That they could be perceived as impertinent or in certain situations as intrusive! One example: an expat had just been transferred to The Hague and was in the middle of giving instructions to the movers, when, out of the blue, an unknown woman barged into the room: 'Hello, I'm your neighbour. Do you have children?' The expat's response: 'I was flabbergasted! Okay, she meant well, but it felt like an unsetting violation of privacy.'

'The most appreciated Dutch meal is an Indonesian rice table.'
(Maria Teresa Cesário, Wageningen University, 1997)

The power of equality

This emphasis on, but also the self-evident nature of *gelijkheid* (equality) in the Dutch culture, together with the (Calvinist) aversion to frills and boasting – in addition to the need for order in this small, flat and overcrowded country – sometimes leads to practice being surprisingly different in the Netherlands.

Along these lines, important foreigners – or those who consider themselves important – could end up feeling offended if they are not, for instance, given preferential treatment in a hospital or if they are not allowed to wait in the VIP-lounge at Amsterdam's Schiphol Airport. Yes, if there is one thing the Dutch truly dislike then it's disparate treatment or special privileges. And therefore at

---

Beleefdheid, bescheidenheid en respect zijn in de opvoeding en opleiding van tegenwoordig ondergeschikt aan het belang dat aan assertiviteit wordt gehecht.
'Courtesy, discretion and respect in rearing and educating nowadays are secondary to the importance attached to assertiveness.'
(Belma Aliagić, Technical University Delft, 2007)

Dutch birthday parties, to the amazement of expats, not only is the person whose birthday it is congratulated, but everybody in the room. 'Oh, it's your birthday, then it's my birthday a little too!', is how the Dutch seem to see it. This also explains why they are so attached to an array of formalities such as arriving on time (being late is considered arrogant). And if you are visiting somewhere, you shake all hands in the room – from the children to the seniors, nobody is excluded. If you want an assistant at your work to do something for you, then you need to ask nicely, I repeat: ask nicely – never issue commands! Orders are unacceptable to the Dutch, who are highly-allergic to hierarchy. This is also the reason the Dutch prefer addressing each other without referring to a person's position or their formal title. And that is also why there are hardly any theatres with (private) loge seating. The Dutch consider such a separate space elitist and therefore unnecessary – explaining why VIPs usually sit with the regular public. For instance, the Dutch queen enjoys going to see dance performances at the Nederlands Danstheater in The Hague. Because there is no loge, others in the audience then see her taking a seat amongst them.

Young people with *allochtoon* backgrounds – raised by parents belonging to dominant immigrant groups (Turkish, Moroccan, Antillean) in the country – have difficulties understanding this aversion to hierarchical relationships and therefore find this hard to accept. These youngsters are accustomed to clear codes of behaviour and visible signs of authority and order and that is not the case here. This can lead to problems.

Those two Dutch words: *autochtoon* and *allochtoon*

In the Netherlands, you will regularly hear the words *autochtoon* and *allochtoon*. These are derived from the Ancient Greek words: *autos* = self; *allos* = other; and *chthon* = ground, land or country – therefore *autochtoon* literally meaning from the country itself and *allochtoon* from another country. The word *allochtoon* was coined in 1971, by the Dutch sociologist Hilda Verwey-Jonker to replace the then commonly-used term immigrant. It was meant to have positive connotations, but with the passing of time it took on negative associations. In fact, nowadays many Dutch people connect the word to things such as not being assimilated into Dutch society; being (the child of) a migrant worker; having a skin colour other than white; not speaking Dutch. For this reason, some politicians want to disallow the use of the word *allochtoon* in official documents.

Confusion also exists about exactly who is *allochtoon* and who is *autochtoon*. The *Centraal Bureau voor de Statistiek* (CBS or Statistics Netherlands) – the agency that collects and provides statistics for governmental policymaking, research and business – defines *allochtoon* as a person with at least one parent who was born abroad. The problem you run into with this designation is that a large part of the population of the Netherlands falls under it – yes, even Queen Beatrix and Prince Willem-Alexander are *allochtoon* according to this description. An *au-*

tochtoon, according to the definition of the CBS, is somebody with two parents who were born in the Netherlands, regardless of the country where that child was born.

❖❖❖

As an expat, you may find the Dutch obsession with equality somewhat annoying. It might even start to irritate you – but it has been this way for centuries and it is not about to change anytime soon. Just try to accept it. It is part and parcel of living in the Netherlands.

❖❖❖

Very Dutch
There are a number of typically Dutch words and terms that express something about the Netherlands and Dutch cultural identity that are 'untranslatable'. Foreigners will regularly come across these words. I have listed a few important ones in alphabetical order below, either indicating the page(s) where this word is explained or followed by a definition:

❖ *Allochtoon*: see p. 38.
❖ *Borrel*: 1 strong alcoholic drink; 2 organising a social gathering, a get-together. The Dutch like to invite each other for a *borrel*. See p. 127.
❖ *Gedogen* (literally to put up with): Turning a blind eye to what is actually prohibited by law. This form of toleration

developed in the Netherlands related to politically controversial issues such as abortion, euthanasia and soft drugs, areas where legislation could not keep pace with sweeping changes in public morality. Jurisdiction and enforcement helped address this by introducing the idea of *gedogen*. For instance, this made it possible – in anticipation of the laws and rules being revised – to not have to prosecute violations in the areas of pornography, age limits for homosexual contact and the use of illegal substances.

However, the word *gedogen* has also taken on something of a negative connotation. It's sometimes associated with laxness, shirking responsibility and keeping silent about certain matters.

- *Gelijkheid* (equality): see p. 36.
- *Gezellig:* see p. 123.
- *Gezin* (family): While most languages have only one word to express the notion of family, the Dutch language actually has two: *gezin,* meaning parents and their child(ren), 'nuclear family' – and *familie,* which includes the *gezin* as well as grandparents, uncles, aunts, nieces, nephews, cousins. For many Christian politicians in the Netherlands, the following credo applies: 'The *gezin* is the cornerstone of the society.' They consider the family to be the smallest form of the church, where it is possible to worship God and hold each other accountable in terms of Christian values. The Christian household is modelled on the Holy Family.

- ❖ *Kapsones* (slang from Yiddish): Airs, arrogance, bragging, pretentiousness, acting like a big shot; pretending to be something that you are not. Generally speaking, the Dutch don't respond well to *kapsones* and this is clearly illustrated by the expression: *Doe maar gewoon, dan doe je al gek genoeg* (Be normal, then you're crazy enough).
- ❖ *Koffietijd* (literally coffee time, also coffee break): see pp. 127, 128. Attention: a coffee shop is not a coffee bar, but a place to buy soft drugs!
- ❖ *Polderen:* solving problems by consensus; discussing end-lessly without daring to make a decision.

❖❖

'The experience of living in a foreign country
makes you better understand your native country.'
(Maris Kuningas, Leiden University, 2007)

MEETING THE DUTCH

THE BASICS

This book takes a good look at Dutch manners. As a foreigner living here, on more than one occasion, you will be confronted with surprising things about etiquette in the Netherlands. Perhaps you will be totally flustered about how you should best react.

To begin with, don't be too hard on yourself because etiquette is actually a lot easier than you think. In fact, the entire system of good manners consists of two basic principles that can essentially be applied all over the world. The rest of the rules, yes all of them – from Spain to Kazakhstan and from Oman to Iceland – reflect these two principles:

1. **Take others into consideration.**
2. **Be absolutely clear.**

Always keep these two principles in mind. And if you end up in an awkward etiquette situation with the Dutch, then depend on your sound judgment and rely on principle(s) #1 and/or #2. This will make your life as an expat much easier. You will see: Etiquette is not hell, but swell!

In practical terms, this means that if you don't understand something (for instance: you are invited for an afternoon drink at the neighbour's house, but you do not know how you should dress, how long it will last, or if there will be anything to eat...) then just go with #2 above and this will ensure clarity. To do this, simply ask for more information. Your neighbour knows you are a foreigner, therefore he or she will not be surprised by your questions, and then you will not have to feel unsure of yourself – resulting in a win-win situation!

Under other circumstances – for instance if you are confronted with behaviour by Dutch people that you think is remarkable or irritating (you drop by unexpectedly at Dutch friends, but they will not let you in; children bouncing off the walls disturb a dinner at the home of friends, etc.) – then remember #1. As I will explain in more detail in this chapter, the Dutch have always had their own idiosyncrasies. Take this into account; accept them as they are. You are a guest in their country and will have to adapt somewhat to them.

And let us not forget: don't be afraid to make mistakes. Once again, you are a foreigner and the Dutch will understand (and forgive), as long as you make it clear that it was not your intention to offend anyone. If you rely on the two basic principles, you actually cannot go wrong. Because as the French are fond of saying: *Politesse passe partout* (Courtesy opens all doors).

These two basic principles clearly illustrate that when it comes to manners and etiquette it is not so much about rigidly hanging onto rules, as it is about having the right mentality – about having a 'fundamentally positive attitude', as Ruud Lubbers, the Dutch prime minister from 1982 until 1993, once voiced. If you are nice to the Dutch, they will be nice to you in return – it's that simple.

The Dutch always shake hands

Greetings

How does contact between people begin? With greetings of course, so that is where I am going to begin too. And that instantly brings us to the significance of the handshake, which surprises many expats. A comment you often hear: 'The Dutch might consider themselves informal, but they think shaking hands is important.' A Polish expatriate tells how each day when she went to pick up her daughter at school, she nodded in a friendly way at the other parents: 'But nobody reacted. They ignored me, as if I didn't exist. This made me feel very uncomfortable. It was only later that I understood that first I had to shake hands with everybody, because only then do people know who you are.'

These Dutch formalities related to shaking hands can also be wrongly interpreted. A group of French people were gathered around a conference table waiting for a Dutch guest speaker. When he arrived, he first went around the table and introduced himself to everyone with a handshake. This is considered customary and po-

Guter Gruß, guter Dank
Wie goed groet, goed ontmoet
Good greetings lead to good meetings

lite in the Netherlands, but the French were surprised: 'This came across as arrogant. In France only the boss – a superior – would shake everyone's hand.'

To be absolutely clear: at a first meeting, you should always give a Dutch man (or woman, as well as a child) your (right) hand. Look someone directly in the eye; do not have your left hand tucked inside your pocket while you are shaking hands. Also shake hands when it is time for you to leave. If you cannot extend your right hand (for instance because it is bandaged) then extend your apologies instead.

And men: always remove your gloves – the right one first – before offering someone your hand. Shaking hands with your gloves on is considered rude even if it is very chilly outside. The impoliteness of not shaking someone's hand skin-to-skin was clearly illustrated during U.S. President George W. Bush's visit to Slovakia in 2005. His unheard of failure to remove his black leather gloves when greeting the country's president was widely publicised.

A handshake is not always required if and when you meet someone for the second time – after all they have already met you. With large groups, you can get away with a simple nod but in a small gathering it is better to greet everybody individually with a handshake. Remember: better to have shaken too many hands than too few. It is also important to look directly at people, also during a conversation.

The host sets the tone

Apart from this, in the Netherlands there are also individuals – mainly Orthodox (religious) Muslims and Jews – who purposely avoid eye contact during a greeting or don't extend their hand. Are you expecting to meet people from these groups? Then remember this as a general rule: Your host or hostess is the one who sets the tone – meaning that he or she establishes the requirements that guests are expected to follow; he/she determines matters such as the timeframe, food and drink, dress code, programme, etc. Guests are expected to accept these 'rules'. Someone who enters a Catholic Church, for instance in Italy, is expected to be dressed appropriately: therefore no bare legs or shoulders. Dutch men in shorts are curtly asked to leave. As a guest in the house of Jesus, you are expected to show respect. Similarly, even Queen Beatrix when she was visiting a mosque in the Netherlands attuned her behaviour to the situation: guests have to remove their shoes and the rules specify that men and women do not shake hands. The queen took no offence with any of this. And two more Royal gestures as examples: In 2007, Prince Willem-Alexander greeted a native Maori who welcomed him to New Zealand with the traditional *Hongi*: rubbing noses together. And while the Emperor of Japan gave Queen Beatrix a firm handshake during his visit to the Netherlands, when the queen travelled to Japan, she bowed in the normal Japanese way. Be a polite guest and follow the lead of your host or hostess. And if you are uncertain about their rules, do not hesitate to ask.

However, if you are meeting people in a public place, then it's a different story – then the rules are not so clear-cut because there is not an obvious host or hostess. Are you feeling insecure about the acceptable forms of greeting or behaving related to the people you will be meeting, etc.? Then it is advisable to consult beforehand, so that misunderstandings, irritations and painful situations can be avoided.

Lastly: the Dutch make little or no distinction between their left and right hand. When they give you something, they do so with whichever hand is free. In some cultures, for example Arabic, the left hand is the lavatory hand and is therefore considered unclean, but the Dutch do not use one particular hand for personal hygiene, praying or eating. Therefore you don't have to be offended if an item is offered with the left hand.

SOCIAL KISSING

From the handshake to the kiss: foreigners are amazed at the amount of kissing that goes on among the Dutch. (Have a quick look at the next infobox!). But first let me add: until recently it was unusual in the Netherlands for men to embrace and/or kiss each other in public. Yet, one sees this more and more these days, in part following similar practices from Southern and Eastern European countries. Even the princes of the Dutch Royal Family, at the

House of Orange weddings over the past years, expressed their mutual affection by openly embracing and kissing each other.

✣✣

Are three kisses obligatory?

The Dutch are a kissy bunch: with a preference for kissing three times and as often as possible. It seems as if everywhere you look, everybody is kissing everyone else, even when the individuals involved barely know each other. This so-called *drieklapper* (3-smacks), a custom originating from the Dutch provinces of Brabant and Limburg to the south, spread rampantly through the country after 1980. Meanwhile, kissing three times has become so commonplace and compulsory that people think this is how it's done. As you might imagine, they are relieved when they hear that all this kiss-kiss-kiss is **not** obligatory. You are still master of your own lips when it comes to this custom. So make the choice yourself... one, two or three kisses. Oh, you don't want to kiss at all? Then, wearing a big smile, assertively extend your hand so the others have to turn themselves inside out to give you a kiss. A firm handshake, while looking someone directly in the eye, is perhaps more intimate and friendly than smacking your lips three times *mwráááh* in the air.

✣✣

Oh yes... avoid greeting someone with a slap on the back, especially the first time you meet them. While such a clap on the shoulder is considered an acceptable sign of friendship in the United States, this is not the case in the Netherlands. Queen Beatrix was hardly amused when President George W. Bush welcomed her in this good ol' Texan way.

On the other hand, the recently fashionable Dutch *wrijfje* – which involves greeting someone by giving their upper arm a quick rub (with or without a handshake) – is acceptable.

INTRODUCTIONS: WHAT'S IN A NAME?

In the Netherlands, you can be introduced by someone or you can take the initiative and introduce yourself. Foreigners find the latter 'unheard of'. They are accustomed to waiting to be introduced to somebody they do not know. In either of these situations, in the Netherlands, it is common practice to say your name when you are shaking hands. Feel free to use your first and last name among friends. In business situations, you can choose to say only your last name. Women usually use both their names. And certainly you can include a polite phrase such as *Hoe maakt u het?* (How do you do?).

Some Dutch people simply say *Aangenaam* (Pleased to meet you). The reply *Aangenaam* was routinely used during Queen Wilhelmina's reign (1898–1948), even by the queen herself. But once the middle class adopted this usage, high-society dropped it. So be careful to whom you say the word *Aangenaam*.

Apart from this, remember that a Dutch woman does not completely relinquish her maiden name when she marries. All official documents (tax papers and ballot papers as well as identity cards and passports) continue to mention a woman's maiden name not only once she's married, but also if she's divorced or widowed. In the Dutch passport, the last name of the husband only appears when this is requested. Of course, in daily life, a woman can use her husband's name – in combination with her own last name or not. However when you are sending a letter to a couple, it should be addressed with both their names (Mr and Mrs Van Gogh-van Ditzhuyzen).

If nobody steps forward to introduce you, then just go ahead and introduce yourself. The following approach applies: at a small gathering (up to about twenty people) you would walk around the room greeting everyone with a handshake, at the same time introducing yourself by name. At a large gathering you should limit yourself to greeting people in your immediate vicinity. But take care: not everybody is equally approachable. You need to be personally introduced to high-placed individuals or *Bekende Nederlanders*, also referred to as *BN'ers* (for instance members of the Dutch Royal House, ministers, CEOs, TV and film stars, media and sports moguls, etc.). In such situations, the initiative must come from the person 'higher in rank', for instance the host/hostess, someone with whom the well-known Dutch person is acquainted, or that *BN*'er him/herself. This always applies! Do not think you can just strike up a conversation with these kinds of important individuals – you may know who they are, but they do not know you.

FORMS OF ADDRESS: INS & OUTS

When a Dutch person introduces him or herself with their first and last name, this does not immediately extend permission for you to address them by their first name. Wait until the other person takes the initiative, and certainly if you hold a 'lower' position or you are in a situation where you need something from them (you are interested in doing business, receiving a subsidy, etc.).

A man is addressed in Dutch as *Meneer* (Mr) plus his last name, a woman as *Mevrouw* (Mrs) without her last name. It stems from the past, when this was done as a sign of discretion – a woman's privacy had to be protected. But nowadays, it's mainly done for practical reasons: in this way preventing confusion related to her name (with the possibility of an unpleasant mistake being made) – since women still change their last names in conjunction with marriage or divorce. Though this practice seems to be decreasing as a result of emancipation, today more and more women are addressed with their last names as well.

On Dutch radio and television nowadays, people are also addressed using both their first and last names, consequently without the addition of Mr or Mrs. This goes as follows: 'Good morning, Vincent van Gogh, could you tell me...', 'Johan Cruijff, what do you think of this?'

Note: young people tend to introduce themselves using only their first names ('Hello, I am Rembrandt') and therefore may be addressed in the same way. However, this does not compel you to do so or to accept the same in return.

Important: Never converse while you are chewing gum. This expresses an attitude of indifference and is consequently impolite.

Esteemed titles and honours

As already mentioned earlier in this book, the Dutch are not fond of pretentious behaviour; they tend to prefer modesty. This means that people do not include titles, honours or ranks (academic, professional, noble) when introducing or addressing someone – except, of course, in the case of the head of state. To her you would say *Majesteit* (Your Majesty; Ma'am is also acceptable). Furthermore, a minister and an ambassador may be addressed as *Excellentie* (Your Excellency) but this is not obligatory. Those holding teaching positions at university are generally addressed as Professor. Noble titles are never voiced aloud; therefore refrain from saying: *Goedemorgen, Graaf Bentinck* (Good morning, Count Bentinck), and also never say: *Mijnheer de Baron* (directly translated: 'Mr Baron') except, perhaps, when you work for him.

This very Dutch aversion to ranks and positions can be difficult for newcomers to make sense of. Particularly when it involves who holds which position in a company or an organisational hierarchy. The status of the person being introduced is, in fact, not always clear. This is in sharp contrast to the customs of other countries, where one would be presented and/or addressed for example as *Ingegnere* (Italian for engineer), *Herr/Frau Generaldirektor* (director of a large company) or *Monsieur le Maire* (Mayor). So make sure you do your work beforehand when you are planning to visit a particular organisation. You can, for instance, inquire in advance about who will be present or find out more about how the organisation is structured. This kind of information is often easily accessible via Internet. Also ask for business cards. Because – thank goodness – titles, honours and ranks are usually included in written and printed materials: on business cards, in letters, e-mails, etc.

Being on a first-name basis
(*Tutoyeren* in Dutch; *duzen* in German; *tutoyer* in French)
In their own language, the Dutch have no qualms about addressing people in an informal way, on a first-name basis. Yet, they also tend to do this when they are speaking German or French. The well-known German newspaper *Frankfurter Allgemeine Zeitung* articulated this inclination of theirs as the Dutch *Duzgesellschaft*. This not only causes confusion and uncertainty with some foreigners, but they often find it rather irritating. A few German and French people

commented: 'From the CEO to the receptionist, the switchboard operator to the cashier, everybody just uses *je* and *jij* (the informal form of you), while it's not always what we prefer.' 'In addition,' they cautioned, 'don't see this informal behaviour (even calling someone by their first name) as a sign of friendship; rock-hard business negotiations simply proceed on course.'

Helpful hint: Whenever you speak Dutch to someone, address all the adults you meet (older than around twenty-one), at least initially, with the formal or polite form of *u* (you). After a while people will often start to introduce you to others in an informal way, using *je* and *jij*. Switching over to this first-name basis should be initiated by the person 'higher up' (your boss, someone older) or by people in a similar situation to yourself (neighbours, colleagues, members of your association). For instance, if as a middle-aged woman you are uninvitedly addressed informally as *je* (informal *you* in Dutch) by a young colleague and you would prefer they refrain from doing this, then continue to speak to them using *u* (formal *you* in Dutch). If they still persist, then just say you would prefer not being *getutoyeerd* (addressed informally).

Finally, a much-asked question: 'When I'm speaking to someone who works in a bookshop, butcher shop or any other kind of store, do I use the polite form of address in Dutch (meaning *u* for you)?' The unequivocal answer is that you use *u*, simply because the use of the informal forms (*je* or *jij* in Dutch) might come across as arrogant or even condescending.

Women and men

Remarkable in the Netherlands is the more or less total equality of men and women. This is also because nowadays it is commonly accepted that Dutch women work, even when they have (young) children. Young Dutch women today work much more than their counterparts of earlier decades. Around fifty-five percent of women ages fifteen to sixty-four have a job for twelve hours or more per week. Dutch women like to work part-time, even when they do not have young children.

Many Dutch people consider the so-called *anderhalfverdieners-model* (essentially 1.5 times a full-time job per family) as the ideal family situation. Dutch women generally work fewer hours (outside the home) than men do and see to the home front and children. This strong preference is specific to the Netherlands. In most other EU countries, the majority of parents like to work full-time. The percentage of Dutch women in top functions is still relatively low, not even ten percent. A striking fact considering that in previous centuries the Netherlands was known as a place where women wore the pants.

So if you are an expat: always take the equality of men and women into consideration. There is also a good possibility that a Dutch woman will take much more initiative than you are used to. Dutch women are also very self-reliant. So if you are a man, do not be surprised if a woman curtly rejects your offer to help her with her coat: 'I'm more than capable of doing that myself!' could very well be the response you get. Mind you, Dutch men who are seated usually do not stand when a woman enters the room. In addition, it is not automatically assumed in restaurants or cafes that the man is the one who pays. People often share the bill (Going Dutch) or the woman pays (if she has extended the invitation).

Also realise that it's still possible that you will end up having a woman as your boss, doctor, police officer, lawyer etc. A woman in any of these positions in the Netherlands would be dealt with exactly the same as her male colleagues. Keep this in mind.

Here follow two examples to illustrate the equality of men and women. A young Afghan manager related a story about when he first moved to the Netherlands: 'I quickly had a Dutch girlfriend and went with her to the disco. Well, she wanted to dance with other men there and naturally I disapproved. In my culture, what a man wants is law. It took an immense effort for me to get used to this equality between men and women.'

The second example is related to a Dutch TV-programme that was broadcast in the early 1990s. A stunning-looking teacher asserted that she could recognise the handwriting of ten of her former male students from when they were youngsters. The Franco-Arabic film star Omar Sharif and the show's host were the jurors. The game started: the beautiful woman was shown one of the handwriting samples and asked for the corresponding name. Then the student concerned (now an adult man) appeared from behind a board. Each had to say yes or no. It went well: candidates one through nine all said yes. But, regrettably, number ten said no, because the answer was wrong. But Omar Sharif saw this differently:

'How can you possibly say no to such a beautiful woman?' he said in a disconcerted tone. In his opinion, the tenth man was obliged to say yes. 'No', the Dutch insisted, that went against the rules and also was not true. 'But', Sharif continued, 'doesn't her beauty outweigh the truth?'

Een groet doet goed, **'A greeting a day...'**
In conclusion: one of the truly upbeat customs in the Netherlands is greeting each other upon arriving at and departing from a shop, your work, on the street (acquaintances), in offices, in doctor's waiting rooms, etc. This is done in Dutch by saying either: *Goedemorgen, Goedemiddag, Goedenavond* (Good morning, Good afternoon, Good evening, for both arriving and departing); *Dag meneer/ mevrouw* (Hello and/or goodbye Sir/Ma'am, also for both arriving and departing); *Tot ziens* (goodbye, only for departing). Many expats are rather astonished by this custom: 'Even if I don't know the people?', they ask. Indeed, but once again this is a big part of the equality model. If you take a seat in a doctor's waiting room without saying anything, others might interpret this as arrogant; it could even cross their minds that you think you're better than they are.

By the way, the use of these traditional Dutch hellos and goodbyes, just mentioned here, seems to be dwindling. They are being pushed aside, in a remarkably rapid tempo, by expressions adopted from the United States such as *Nog een fijne dag verder, Een fijne avond* and *Een fijn weekend* (Have a nice day, a nice evening, a nice

| Index finger | Index finger | Raised |
| on the forehead | on the temple | index finger |

weekend) – with people expressing the latter as early as Thursday afternoon. One is bombarded with these catchphrases in shops and on television; the result being that many Dutch people have now taken to using them as well. But all is not lost: you may safely continue saying *Goedemorgen* or *Tot ziens*.

And last but not least: at some point you'll undoubtedly hear somebody cheerfully utter *Doei!* (pronounced: doo-ey) or *Doeg!* (pronounced: doogh) – two Dutch goodbyes that have gained in popularity over the last thirty years. *Doei* is originally a greeting in a dialect spoken in the Zaanstreek, an area north of Amsterdam. It is a version of the word *doeg*, from the Dutch word *dag* (used for both hello and goodbye), also meaning *goedendag* (literally good day). But watch out! Though *doei* and *doeg* are acceptable in certain settings, they are best to avoid at the office or for formal occasions.

✦✦

Those Dutch gestures: Three fingers & two hands

1. **Index finger on the forehead**: When a Dutch person *tiks* (taps) his or her index finger in the middle of their forehead above their nose, this means that something or someone is very strange and/or completely idiotic (thus literally *getikt* or nuts).
2. **Index finger on the temple:** When a Dutch person places their index finger just above their left or right temple, then they think something or someone is clever.

3. **Raised index finger:** The Dutch are renowned for thinking they know everything better. With their (symbolic) admonishing finger, harking back to the strict sermons given by Calvinist ministers, they thrive on telling other countries how to conduct their affairs.

4. **Waving the left or right hand beside the cheek:** indicates yummy or *lekker* (delicious)!

5. **Turning the left or right hand back and forth (height of the chest):** means hmmm... something is dubious.

✧✧

Een goede buur is beter dan een verre vriend
Mieux vaut un voisin proche qu'un frère éloigné
Ein guter Nachbar an der Hand ist besser als ein
Freund über Land
You can live without your friends, but not without your neighbours

CONTACT WITH THE NEIGHBOURS:
FROM GETTING TO KNOW YOU TO THE 11 P.M. RULE

The saying below left, common to several different languages, clearly illustrates the importance of having good contact with your neighbours. And it certainly applies when it comes to expatriates. Consequently, a few helpful hints follow here:

* Introduce yourself by dropping a friendly card in the mailbox. Include who you are, what you do and invite them over for coffee, tea or a drink. Do not say *Kom eens langs* (Come by some time), but suggest a specific time and date. Handiest is to invite all your neighbours together (those living to the right, left, across the street if desired, upstairs and downstairs). If the first visit goes well, your neighbours will invite you over to their places, so that each of you gets a chance to see the other person's home.

* Give each other a hand the first time you meet. Afterwards routinely greet your neighbours when you leave or arrive home, on the staircase, or on the street with a brief *Goedemorgen* (Good morning) or *Hallo* (Hello).

* Inform your neighbours – verbally or in writing – if you are going to throw a party, go on holiday or if you are planning to renovate your house. This could prevent ending up at odds with each other.

* It's handy to exchange house keys. This way, in your absence, your neighbours can intervene in case of an emergency (fire,

robbery, etc.). In addition, many neighbours care for each other's houseplants and/or garden if the other people are away or ill.

- ❖ Prevent irritations: Don't park your car in your neighbour's space.
- ❖ Keep the pavement in front of your house clean. Everybody is obliged to do this. Shovel the snow and scatter sand or salt if it is icy weather.
- ❖ Avoid causing your neighbours any inconvenience. The Dutch live somewhat on top of each other (the average population density being 450 people per square kilometre) and therefore are more easily irritated by the conduct of others. This is a good reason to limit the volume of your radio, stereo speakers and television; make sure your children are not continuously running around and/or exuberantly making noise; and do not make a BBQ or light a fire late at night – the penetrating odour could easily annoy the people who have gardens or balconies nearby your house.

Along with all of this, always keep the 11 p.m. rule in mind. Meaning: after this hour you are expected not to make any noise (droning music, shouting guests, working with power tools, etc.). So do not be surprised if an irritated neighbour rings your bell around this time asking if you could quiet it down, while you just sank into a comfortable chair to enjoy the warmth of an outdoor fire with an inspiring piece of music.

DRESSED TO KILL?

Hmm, what can one safely say about how the Dutch dress? We generally evaluate people we are meeting for the first time based on their outward appearance. So it's important to note that the dress code here is considerably more nonchalant than in other European countries. Many foreigners simply can't believe their eyes. As early as 1882, the French founder of an Amsterdam high-fashion house was heard to moan: 'I thought I'd landed in China, so awful, so estranged from any comprehension of fashion, was how the ladies here dressed.' And the Duke of Baena – who served as the ambassador of Spain in the Netherlands from 1956 to 1964 – found the Dutch tendency to deliberately behave in a simple way, as well as dress very plainly, rather odd. Not only was the country as flat a pint of stale ale, according to him, but socially speaking it was just as flat. The Dutch are obsessed with equality and reject every form of superiority. Dressing stylishly in formal attire, a skirt or even a smart suit is considered a sign of status, something out of the ordinary. Away with this nonsense!

The astonishment expressed by foreigners long ago has also carried over to the present-day: 'In the summertime, Dutch men actually go to dinner in restaurants wearing shorts', commented a horrified Austrian now living here, 'and Dutch women don't wear high heels.' Well, at least in terms of this last remark Princess Máxima is setting a good example. A French man also complained: 'The Dutch go to classical concerts in jeans...! I felt hopelessly overdressed in my suit.'

Dutch footgear is also a cause for alarm. 'The Dutch always wear sneakers.' Or, just as awful, shoes with thick rubber soles ('Very shocking', according to the British). Two Germans who have lived here for a long time were kind enough to share their observations. Journalist Helmut Hetzel: 'In the Netherlands you can often tell from a man's footwear if he's Dutch. Do his socks match his suit? With Dutch men, the combination is often a bit off.' And writer Christoph Buchwald: 'During a debate, it struck me that the shoes of most of the Dutch men looked incredibly worn out: no form, no colour, no upkeep, zilch. They were also dressed rather slovenly compared to the others.' And as if that is not enough, Dutch men sometimes even wear white socks with suits.

But there are Dutch people as well who are irritated by the way their compatriots dress. Someone told me about a festive dinner, in an elegant restaurant, where a group of men showed up wearing denim jeans. 'I feel relaxed in casual clothing', came one response. 'They just have to accept me as I am', followed another. This immediately leads me to ask if we would have to accept this man 'as he is', if he also enjoyed eating with his legs spreadeagle on the table?

How are you, as a foreigner living in the Netherlands, supposed to dress? Well you certainly don't have to take to wearing sneakers everywhere. A good general rule is: you will look fine if your clothes are tidy – no stains, creases or holes – and appropriate for the occasion. Therefore: sporty attire at the beach, smart (suits) at the office, white or black tie (gentlemen) and long dresses (ladies) for an evening gala.

In official social circles, the usual dress codes apply. Have you received an invitation without instructions on how to dress and you are not sure what would be appropriate? Do not hesitate to call your host or hostess. And keep this in mind: overdressed is better then underdressed.

Business dress: Office attire in the Netherlands is fairly conservative, but varies depending on the industry. Bankers, lawyers, and public servants wear suits with ties; today you see more and more women dressed in so-called power suits. While, on the other hand, some fields (advertising, media, IT companies) allow for very casual attire.

Oddly enough, high-placed individuals sometimes dress in a more nonchalant way than people employed under them. And in left-wing and/or progressive Dutch circles, important men have a

---

Observatie van bellen in het openbaar heeft duidelijk gemaakt,
dat GSM staat voor Grote Schijt aan Manieren.
'Observing telephoning in public clearly indicates
that GSM stands for "don't Give a Shit about Manners".'
(C. van Karnebeek, University of Amsterdam, 2002)

---

fondness for appearing at public functions without a tie. Are they trying to impress upon us that they are just regular blokes, without pretentions? This casual approach to dressing has been known to backfire. An expat arrived at a town hall for an official presentation her (large) company was going to give. To her amazement the two Dutch (male) aldermen showed up in casual clothes, while their staff members were smartly dressed.

Finally: your country's national attire may be worn for any occasion, from street fairs to galas, at home and even to meet the queen.

'If you're overdressed you feel ridiculous, if you're underdressed you are ridiculous.' (Dutch fashion designers Viktor & Rolf)
(Marnix Jansen, Utrecht University, 2008)

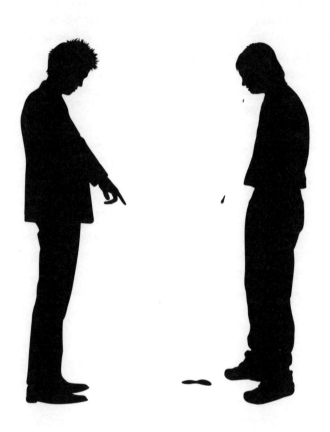

3

Conduct away from home

The way the Dutch conduct themselves outside the house isn't all that different from what goes on elsewhere. However, there are particular practices that cannot be overlooked.

Street-side view – At the beach – In public places

The Dutch generally stay to the right in shopping districts or pedestrian areas, so that the two-way flow of pedestrians can proceed without disturbing each other. 'I think it's terrific!' a Spanish woman exclaimed happily. 'In many other countries you have to clear a path between the busy shoppers and a mass of people who are all talking and walking in different directions.' This once again confirms, according to her, how orderly and responsive to formalities the Dutch are. So adhere to this practice and stroll with the flow of the pedestrian traffic.

On the pavement, it's different. If two people are coming towards you at a rapid pace, consider the possibility that they may not step aside for you, so then you will have to pass them by stepping into the street.

And finally: do not spit on the street! Though this might be acceptable in certain cultures, it's considered a filthy habit in the Netherlands and consequently perceived as extremely bad-mannered.

Fur: Be forewarned about wearing (real) fur stoles, fur hats and especially fur coats when you go out. In the Netherlands there is quite a lot of controversy related to wearing fur, because – according to the banners of animal activists – it's a vile luxury product that causes an immense amount of animal suffering. *Bont is moord!* (Fur is murder!) is one of the popular slogans, as well as *Respect voor Dieren!* (Respect for Animals!). Because of the continuous negative publicity and fanatical protesters in front of clothing shops, some fashion houses have felt obliged to stop selling items that include fur.

This is remarkable, as the Netherlands is the third largest producer of mink in the world, after Denmark and China. Politicians are considering prohibiting this successful branch of business. According to proponents of such a ban, a fur coat is not a vital necessity and there are other alternatives. Indeed, the Dutch have an immense fondness for animals; so much so that the rights of animals now have full-time representation in the halls of parliament: the *Partij voor de Dieren* (Party for the Animals) received two seats in the Dutch parliamentary elections of 2006.

In any case, this means that it can be foolish to go prancing about in a flashy fur coat (real fur of course). This hatred of fur has been known to go so far that activists shout offensive slurs at you; even splash your costly coat or stole with paint or ruin it in some other way. But in comparison to Amsterdam, your furry wrap will be better accepted in The Hague: home to the country's government as well as many international dignitaries, the city's atmosphere is more sophisticated.

AT THE BEACH

For many expats, the close proximity of the sea, with its dunes and beaches, is an attractive aspect of living in the Netherlands. However, be aware of the fact that Dutch sun worshippers are fond of hanging around in as little clothing as possible, also in the *strandtenten* (large cafes with outdoor terrace) along the boardwalks and beaches. Dutch men are not embarrassed about having a hanging beer belly, a bad figure or – for that matter – wearing the most minuscule swimsuit. Women sunbathe topless without inhibition, even with sagging breasts and – if at all possible – wearing a string bikini. Heterosexual and homosexual pairs alike openly embrace without giving Peeping Toms a second thought.

Do you think all this nakedness and free-thinking behaviour is simply too much? Then you best look for a beach that is not so busy; there are enough of these to be found. But take care that you don't mistakenly end up on a nudist beach. Many foreigners are shocked when during a pleasant (family) stroll on the beach they bump into a bunch of nudists. Or even worse: if they witness these nudists running and jumping, playing badminton and volleyball. The Dutch, on the other hand, think all of this is perfectly normal. So if you find this disagreeable, inquire in advance about the locations of such nudist beaches. Apart from this, dogs are not allowed on most beaches during the day.

In public places

(Locker rooms of) saunas, swimming pools, health clubs: These kinds of facilities are frequently mixed – with men and women using the same space at the same time. Do you find this objectionable? Then remember to ask in advance how this is arranged. When it comes to co-ed locker rooms, you might prefer to change at home before and after exercising.

Shopping: It is not the practice in shops in the Netherlands to bargain about the price of goods. Items have a fixed price and what something costs is simply non-negotiable.

Moving staircases (escalators) in train stations, shops, etc.: The Dutch take up a lot of space on escalators; they often stand side-by-side blocking the passage of others. This can be exasperating for people who are trying to catch a train, so the Dutch Railway Company has started a campaign entitled *Houd rechts op de roltrap* (Keep right on the escalator). Do you often find yourself trying to pass people as well? Then politely ask those in front of you if you might get by them. Fortunately, they usually comply.

Opera, theatre, concerts
Some more characteristic things about the behaviour of the Dutch follow... again so you won't be taken by surprise:
* **Sloppy attire:** The Dutch are not in the habit of dressing up to attend the theatre, but often show up in their so-called daily

gear. This is also another illustration of that Dutch saying *Doe maar gewoon* (Be normal). The Italian, Riccardo Chailly, former conductor of the *Koninklijk Concertgebouworkest*, found this not only annoying, but totally rude. Chailly: 'It wouldn't have surprised me if the Dutch showed up at the opera in their underwear!'

You are certainly not obliged to imitate the Dutch in this respect. Go ahead and dress festively. Not only will you feel good about yourself, but it also shows respect for the performers, musicians and other artists who are there doing their very best to entertain you.

- **Coughing:** The Dutch cough and sneeze during concerts and opera performances without any restraint. All this *ahem, ahem* and *achoo* is extremely distracting. 'I offer you my apologies for the coughing', said the director of Amsterdam's *Koninklijk Concertgebouworkest*, Simon Reinink, blushing from embarrassment, to pianist Alfred Brendel after his farewell recital in October 2008. So do not be surprised if you are subjected to a concert of coughing. And please don't take part. But what if you abruptly have to cough? Breathe deeply, swallow hard and/or suck ferociously on a lozenge or a peppermint.

- **Standing ovations:** There is a remarkable phenomenon in the Netherlands that involves everyone in the audience springing to their feet and starting to clap the minute a performance has ended. It seems as if no distinctions are made – it's not at all related to whether the performance was awful, mediocre, good or superb...it's standing ovationitis! Or perhaps just another example of the Dutch obsession with equality. If you prefer to stay seated, by all means do! Although you will be staring at rows and rows of backs...

- **Quickly getting your coat:** Despite these standing ovations, many concert-goers are still in a hurry to grab their coats. In the case of the *Koninklijk Concertgebouworkest* in Amsterdam, the hall is often half empty within minutes of the final chord being played. And sometimes as the conductor is descending the famous stairs to the podium to take a second bow, he even finds himself fighting the public rushing off to the cloakroom.

❖❖

That Dutch standing ovation

The Australian Simon Murphy, conductor and artistic leader of the New Dutch Academy (NDA), a baroque orchestra in The Hague, adores a standing ovation, that is if it is sincere: 'I'm really honoured, when it happens to me outside the Netherlands.'

He cites three reasons why the Dutch always stand to applaud:

1. To prove they made the correct choice; their good taste demands the performance be a success.
2. The Dutch want value for money. It has got to be first-rate if they paid.
3. Immediately springing to their feet to clap speeds up the process of retrieving their coat.

❖❖

TIPPING

Is tipping required? According to one person it isn't really necessary, according to another it is. And if so: how much? To whom? When? Many Dutch think it goes against the idea of human dignity (and equality) to compensate someone extra for their work. The recipients of these tips tend not to agree: they are more than happy taking a tip. In many countries, such as the United States and Russia, people tend to be generous tippers. This is not the Dutch way and also why they have a reputation as being 'stingy'.

Some rules of thumb: Hotel doormen and/or porters get fifty-euro cents or one euro for every piece of baggage brought to the room. You should leave approximately five per cent of the room price for the chambermaid(s), that is if you stay more than one night and your room is neatly tidied up. When you deliver your coat to a cloakroom you can leave the attendant fifty-euro cents or one euro. In terms of taxi drivers, the tip is generally included. Therefore, you are not required to tip unless the driver is particularly kind and helpful. For staff serving you in cafes and/or restaurants, you may leave a gratuity ranging from five to ten percent of the bill, if you are really satisfied with the service. In 1988, the tip system in the *horeca* (Dutch hotel, restaurant and cafe trade) was done away with, so that prices now include service. So whatever extra you leave, is a true tip. If you pay with a credit card or debit card, then give the tip in cash so the person who served you actually gets the money. Or throw some money in the tip pot, which you find in many establishments. The collected amount is then divided amongst the entire staff. If you don't have any cash with you, when you pay the bill you can add an amount on top. Never ask for change from a tip. And do not tip someone with a pack of gum or chocolate. Yet, what applies unconditionally: if the service was not very good – or heaven forbid: it was awful – then that tip should stay in your wallet.

Lastly, never tip the owner.

MANNERS ON THE GO

'Today, once again, there are traffic jams hundreds of kilometres long.' It's worth repeating: the Netherlands is not only small and flat, but most of the country is densely populated. And this leads to scores of traffic jams.

Though here I must add something about the remarkable past of this country. It has produced a circle of cities that are located a relatively short distance from each other. This in contrast to most other countries, where there is one specific city that serves as the capital, generally a metropolis with one or more millions of inhabi-

---

Savoir conduire, c'est d'abord savoir se conduire
Knowing how to drive, means first knowing how to behave
(Jacques Gandouin, French protocologist, 1972)

tants. The most important institutions are usually concentrated in a capital city: the government, ministries, embassies, large companies, universities, opera, etc. Cities that are smaller and with fewer inhabitants are scattered throughout the rest of a country. However, this is different in the Netherlands. For centuries, this country was mainly governed at the local level. In the Middle Ages, a number of cities became prosperous and powerful. Later on, the country became a true Republic, comprised of seven independent provinces, each with its own capital city.

The Dutch Revolt of 1568–1648

The Netherlands as we know it today, under the rule of the Habsburg Emperor Charles V (1500–1558), was part of a larger territory known as the Burgundian-Habsburg dominion. The first step towards establishing an independent state was taken in 1568 when a number of provinces rebelled against Charles' son Philip II of Spain, their sovereign ruler at the time. This revolt, led by Prince William of Orange – who has gone down in Dutch history as the 'Father of the Netherlands' – marked the beginning of the Eighty Years' War. This finally ended with the signing of the Peace Treaty of Munster (1648), which also recognised the Republic of the Seven United Provinces as an independent state.

Many of these early cities grew in population and expanded, resulting in the west of the Netherlands finally developing into one large patchwork quilt of cities, also referred to as the *Randstad*. But the Netherlands does not have a single uncontested metropolis with everything that accompanies this, such as London (7 million inhabitants), Paris (more than 2 million), Moscow (more than 10 million) or Stockholm (1.6 million). Things have more or less been divided between three relatively small cities: Amsterdam (capital, universities, opera, concert hall and the like; 750,000 inhabitants), The Hague (government seat with all the activities that go with this, many international institutions; 475,000 inhabitants) and Rotterdam (harbour, university; 580,000 inhabitants).

The atmosphere and ambience of these three cities differ significantly:

- Amsterdam is progressive, hip and pro-Republic. Many intellectuals live there (preferably in the *grachtengordel*, 'canal district'), as well as artists and young people, also because of the two universities.
- The Hague is conservative, monarchist, international and *deftig*, 'sophisticated' (government officials, diplomats).
- Rotterdam is proud of its hard workers, the no-nonsense attitude and its *havenbaronnen* (the harbour's captains of industry).

The Italian writer Edmondo de Amicis (1848–1908) wrote at length about the Netherlands in the 19th century: 'At Rotterdam fortunes are made; at Amsterdam they are consolidated; at The Hague they are spent.'

Since the *Randstad* is actually one large city – that is in terms of the traffic – much like Paris or Vienna, you would expect there to be a vast underground railway network. But unfortunately this is not the case. Amsterdam, The Hague and Rotterdam (oops, let's not forget Utrecht here) all have their own transport companies. Luckily, this is being improved upon and the trains that connect these cities now run more frequently.

In the car

The usual traffic rules apply in the Netherlands. And obviously, this small book cannot delve into all of these regulations, but I do want to quickly mention a few important ones: people drive on the right, wearing a seatbelt is mandatory and only hands-free calling is permitted when you are behind the wheel of a car.

Be careful: Emptying a full ashtray, or dumping tins or other rubbish out of your car window is illegal in the Netherlands. This also applies to those so-called travelling boom boxes: setting your car stereo or radio on full-blast and driving around with the music pounding. Do not do this, because you will probably be fined.

Planning to get into your car and drive home after a party or a cheerful dinner? Then take part in the so-called Bob-campaign. The 'Bob' is the person who doesn't drink any alcohol if you are going out on the town. Then he or she can safely chauffeur their friends or colleagues home. When you are making plans away from home, agree in advance on who is going to drive and therefore will not be drinking. And if you cannot reach an agreement with people, plan on calling a taxi or using public transport.

The hope is that this campaign will help decrease alcohol consumption. Drinking is a contributing factor to around fifteen percent of all traffic accidents. Some say that the word Bob is short for **Bewust Onbeschonken Bestuurder** (Consciously Unintoxicated Driver) but it's just a name. The idea of the Bob actually originated in Belgium.

On the bicycle

If there is one thing that is typically Dutch, then it has got to be the bicycle. The vast number of bikes on the road is something that all foreigners notice immediately. However, the bicycle is not a Dutch invention. The fathers of the bicycle, as we know it, were a German and a Frenchman. Carl Baron von Drais von Sauerbronn (1785–1841) first constructed a *vélocipède* (walking bicycle) in 1816. Ten years later, people were already velocipeding in the Netherlands. Even the nobleman Willem Boreel, who later became Speaker of the Lower House of the Dutch Parliament, owned a vélocipède. But it was far from ideal. It wasn't that fast and it was quite tiring. Consequently, the Frenchman Ernest Michaux (1842–1882) invented a pedal cycle. A Dutchman named Otto Frederik Baron Groeninx van Zoelen was the first proud owner in 1867.

By then the bicycle was unstoppable. Everybody went cycling! It also contributed to the emancipation of women – cycling demonstrated that women could be the equals of men; it increased their freedom and made them more independent. The young Dutch Queen Wilhelmina (1880–1962) also became an enthusiast. She purchased a bicycle in Vienna and loved to ride it whenever she had the opportunity. But the government felt this was too dangerous, because 'she was responsible for the well-being of many' and she was no longer permitted to cycle (1897). Still, the queen became an active cyclist later in her life. And even today, members of the Royal Family gladly cycle.

The bicycle is a fact of life in the Netherlands. However, it's also important to realise that the Dutch behave differently on a bicycle from other bikers throughout the world. The Dutch approach to bicycling clearly illustrates how prevailing the notion of *alles moet kunnen* (anything goes) is: they cycle on the pavement; ignore the stoplights; bike with three or even more people side-by-side; ride at night without a front or back light, so you basically can't see them at all... To put it mildly, there are a lot of cyclists who exhibit reckless behaviour. And if the police want to issue them a fine for one of their offences, then the Dutch initiate the usual discussion; blurting out something along the lines of: *Ga toch boeven vangen!* (Go catch some real criminals!). Because, yes, even in the presence of the police, this obsession with equality comes into play: the Dutch do not take kindly to authority; to people telling them what they may and may not do. This is in sharp contrast to other countries, where the police are accorded more respect.

Apart from all this, riding a bicycle has many advantages. It is fast, fun, cheap, healthy and you never have to look for parking space. But because you need to get used to cycling, in the beginning it can also be dangerous. Some helpful hints to avoid accidents:

- Practice a lot before venturing out into the busy traffic.
- Stick to routes with separate bicycle lanes (luckily there are loads).
- Staying balanced is important – therefore hold on tightly to the handlebars with both hands.
- Don't bicycle too close to the kerb.
- As a pedestrian, never walk on a bicycle lane.
- No matter where you are, always remember to lock your bicycle securely and preferably with two sturdy locks. It's unfortunate, but especially in the *Randstad* – and Amsterdam in particular – countless numbers of bikes are regularly stolen. Luckily, there are now lots of affordable *fietsenstallingen* (bicycle shelters) in large Dutch cities.
- In some cities, but again particularly in Amsterdam, you are not permitted to lock your bicycle wherever you like. That's because the use of the bicycle as a means of transport has increased exponentially over the past fifteen years. In Amsterdam alone, the number of bicycles in the city centre has grown by around sixty percent. So sometimes you are required to leave your bike locked in an area specifically designated to 'park' bicycles.
- Watch out for lorries! On a bicycle or moped you may not always be visible to the driver. Even though they glance in their mirrors to check if someone is riding beside or behind them, this does not always guarantee that they will see you. You might

be in their so-called *dode hoek* (literally dead angle). In recent years, due to this blind spot, quite a few (young) people have been seriously injured or killed by trucks turning right.

❖ And never imitate the reckless bicycle-behaviour of the Dutch.

Once you have discovered the bicycle, you will never want to be without one, as the cheerful testimonial 'I love my bike' on the next page illustrates.

'The fact that most Dutch citizens speak English is comfortable for the initial integration of foreigners to the country, but in the end it isolates them from Dutch culture.'
(M. Quesada Vilar, Leiden University, 2007)

✥✥

I love my bike!

According to the Netherlands Association for the Bicycle and Automobile Industry (RAI) an estimated 18 million bicycles are used regularly in the Netherlands. Riding a bike is a way to totally immerse yourself in the Dutch culture.

- ✥ I love my bike because it allows me to explore neighbourhoods and hidden streets in my adopted city. It allows me to bypass cars stuck in traffic during rush hour.
- ✥ I love my bike because it gives me a chance to breathe fresh air while enjoying green scenery.
- ✥ I love my bike because it keeps me moving.
- ✥ I love my bike because it makes me feel I am more a part of Dutch society.
- ✥ Everyday, I join thousands of Dutch citizens on their bicycles heading off to school, to work, or to visit friends and family.

Olivia Neri (Travel writer, Los Angeles) in the expat magazine
ACCESS (Autumn 2008)

✥✥

IV

GETTING IN TOUCH WITH THE DUTCH

Communicating with the Dutch occurs in all kinds of ways: written and verbal, for both private and business matters. Here you will find some important things to keep in mind. And since contact is initiated and maintained via language, that is where I will begin.

SPREEKT U NEDERLANDS?, 'DO YOU SPEAK DUTCH?'

'Why should I bother to learn Dutch? Everybody speaks English here,' an expat remarked. Another said: 'Ugh, the Dutch language. With all those throaty *ggg*s, it sounds as if they are always gargling.' A third expat basically thought Dutch was too difficult to learn, especially given the limited amount of time she was going to live in the Netherlands.

All right, there are reasons enough to give up on the Dutch language. Yet, I was still able to come up with seven reasons to invest energy in exploring this language of the place where you are now living:

1. **Because it is polite:** Showing an interest in the language of your host country is congenial and gracious.
2. **Because it is useful:** You will be able to read signboards, you can eavesdrop on the people around you, you will be able to follow the media (newspapers, radio, TV), etc. Every bit of the Dutch

you master will increase your understanding of Dutch culture and therefore your appreciation for the country. And besides: the linguistic centre of your brain will be also stimulated.

3. **Because it is charming:** You will make a good impression if you speak *een beetje Nederlands* (a bit of Dutch).

4. **Because it is important:** Poor language skills make it difficult to find a job or suitable childcare and to deal with the administrative bureaucracy in the Netherlands.

5. **Because it is fun:** You will fit in faster and it will be easier to make new friends.

6. **Because it is beautiful:** Yes, I mean it! Each and every language (therefore also Dutch) has its own unique beauty and strength.

7. **Because it is there for the taking...**

Conclusion: why not give it your best shot? Or at least learn some standard Dutch expressions and phrases by heart. And make it a habit of using Dutch to say *Goedemorgen* (Good morning) or *Goedemiddag* (Good afternoon) in shops, offices, waiting rooms, etc. It takes a small effort and you will be perceived as friendly. Do you need to ask somebody something on the street? Don't immediately blurt out your question in English. You might irritate the person you're addressing or they may not understand you. Therefore, learn an opening line in Dutch, such as *Mag ik u iets vragen? Spreekt u Engels?* (May I ask you something? Do you speak English?) and continue in English, of course based on the response.

And what if you cannot manage a single word of Dutch? Then

begin by saying: 'Sorry, I don't speak Dutch, but perhaps you can help me?' This is a good way to break the ice and will make communicating easier.

But,

    but,

        but...

...then there is that huge 'but' you hear from expats about barely getting a chance to practice their Dutch, even at an elementary stage. 'When you try to speak Dutch', said a Dane, 'they immediately cut you off and switch to English, in essence shutting you out.' Another irritated expat added: 'In shops, I always do my best to speak Dutch and then they reply in English, as if to say "My English is better than your Dutch". So I just avoid these shops.'

Perhaps you have experienced this problem too, because it is a complaint I heard again and again. So if you want to continue conversing in Dutch, you will have to make this absolutely clear. Tell people you are trying to learn the language and want to practice as much as possible (otherwise you are never going to learn it). In this case, most Dutch people will be happy to oblige.

Note: your beginner's knowledge of Dutch might easily lead to amusing miscommunications. An Asian manager once wanted to have his house painted. The painter arrived and said he wanted to do it *zwart* (black). '*Zwart?*' the manager questioned. 'But I was thinking of yellow and white!' (*Zwart* here meaning 'under the table'. He wanted to be paid in cash so the tax authorities would not find out about the transaction.) And then there was a Spaniard with

Jehovah's Witnesses at his door saying that they *licht kwamen bren-gen* (literally came to bring light). The man replied: 'But I already have five lamps!' (except in this case they meant light as a message of Salvation).

❖❖

About *koetjes en kalfjes*, 'cows and calves'

The Netherlands is cow country! Fat, shiny, grazing cows are inseparable from the Dutch landscape. The black and white Friesian dairy cow is world-famous and the province of Friesland is known as the finest of dairy country. Thanks to all these cows, it is possible for the Dutch (and foreigners as well) to enjoy a wealth of dairy products such as cheese, butter, milk, yogurt, *vla* (Dutch custard) and the like. The cow's immense significance to the culture is also illustrated by a variety of Dutch sayings such as *over koetjes en kalfjes praten* (literally talking about cows and calves). This actually means talking about unimportant everyday stuff or small talk – probably best reflected by the English expressions 'chewing the cud' or 'chewing the fat'. Some more cow, cheese and butter related sayings follow here, along with a few in the Frisian language (second official language after Dutch):

❖ *De koe bij de hoorns vatten*, literally 'grabbing a cow (bull) by the horns' or thoroughly tackling something difficult.

- *Een waarheid als een koe*, literally 'a truth like a cow' or something that is self-evident.
- *Bûter, brea en griene tsiis, wa't dat net sizze kin is gjin oprjochte Fries!*, 'Butter, bread and green cheese, whoever cannot pronounce this phrase is not a true Frisian!'
- *In stik bûter yn 'e brij*, literally 'a pat of butter in the porridge' or a windfall or a stroke of good luck.

✧✧

Means of communicating

Telephoning: *U spreekt met Rembrandt van Rijn,* 'You're speaking to Rembrandt van Rijn'

When you ring someone on the telephone, always begin by stating your last name, with or without your first name (and if necessary the name of your company), even if you are calling to speak to somebody besides the person who answers. This also applies – to the surprise of foreigners – to impersonal calls such as ordering a taxi or a pizza, asking for information, etc. You say, for instance, in Dutch (using the polite form): *U spreekt met Rembrandt van Rijn. Kan ik meneer Van Gogh spreken?* (You are speaking to Rembrandt van Rijn. May I speak to Mr Van Gogh?) Or: *U spreekt met Rembrandt van Rijn. Kunt u mij zeggen of er nog kaartjes te koop zijn voor uw concert?* (You are speaking to Rembrandt van Rijn. Can you tell me if there are still tickets available for the concert?) Also be aware that neglecting telephone operators, secretaries or housemates by immediately asking for the actual person you are calling, without first stating who you are, is considered impolite.

Somebody rings you? Then the same applies: you pick up the receiver and clearly state your name (possibly adding your first name or company's name). Only saying *Hallo* (Hello) offhandedly when answering is considered somewhat rude by the Dutch. Though, from time to time, you may get a Dutch person on the line who wants to remain anonymous for privacy reasons. In place of his or her name, they might state their phone number or say *Ja?* (Yes?) or alternatively *Halló?* (Hello?) in a questioning tone.

It is preferable when calling or being called to avoid using only your first name: *Met Vincent!* (Vincent speaking!) One could think: which Vincent? I know at least three. And steer clear of using: *Met mij* (It's me).

Calling via mobile telephone is more relaxed, partly because of the individual nature of these phones. The name of the person who is ringing also often appears on the screen.

Stoor ik?, 'Am I disturbing you?': When you ring, make sure you are not interrupting something. There's nothing more unpleasant than being called by somebody at a bad moment and he or she immediately dives into a long story without inquiring if you have the time. And when it is an inconvenient time, then simply say so. You can also offer to return that person's call at a later moment.

Times not to ring: It is best to call someone after 9 a.m. and no later than 10 p.m. On Sundays you should not ring anybody before 12 noon. It's also better not to interrupt people when they are eating (12 noon to 2 p.m. and 6 p.m. to 7.30 p.m.). Finally: try not to call in the evening between 8 p.m. and 8.30 p.m., as many Dutch people like to watch the evening news on television without being disturbed.

Do not forget: take time differences into account when you are calling from abroad.

Personal contact: Making new friends

According to many expatriates, it is difficult to establish initial contact with the Dutch, especially if you do not have school going children or a Dutch partner. On the other hand, expats also say that once you get to know them better, Dutch people can become reliable and cherished friends. But how do you actually go about doing this? You feel like such an outsider and want to feel like you belong. Some tips follow here:

- Join some kind of a club or organisation (hockey, tennis, bridge, etc.) and actively participate in committees, tournaments etc.
- When conversing with Dutch people, express interest in their country. Many cities and neighbourhoods have a *buurthuis* (a community centre) where all kinds of activities are organised for local residents: lectures, exhibitions, gatherings, morning coffee, etc. Find out if there is such a centre in your neighbourhood.

- At *borrels* (informal get-togethers with drinks and snacks), meetings and other kinds of gatherings avoid the tendency expats have of only talking to each other; actively seek out contact with the Dutch people who are present.
- Are you religious? Join a Dutch church, synagogue, or mosque.
- Make an effort to meet your neighbours – to the left and right, upstairs, downstairs, across the street – and maintain good relations with them.
- Invite Dutch people over to your home. A Bulgarian student attending college in The Hague related: 'I think it's very important to seek out Dutch friends – my suggestion is *integreren* (assimilate) as opposed to *isoleren* (separate). I recently cooked a Bulgarian meal for some of my classmates, and now I have been invited to eat a typically Dutch meal by a girl I have gotten to know.'
- At the office, strike up a conversation with your Dutch colleagues as often as possible. Invite them over to your home for dinner or a drink. Attend interesting gatherings and lectures. Actively participate in company festivities, for example drinking coffee together to celebrate a colleague's birthday; going out for a drink after work and office outings; celebrating the Dutch holiday of St. Nicholas or Christmas, etc. Join a business club.

So possibilities galore! And that's also another reason to learn *een beetje Nederlands* (a bit of Dutch).

Take to the ice!

After a few freezing cold days, the Dutch are felled by so-called *schaatskoorts* (literally skating fever); they long to go skating on natural ice. This has been going on for centuries. An amazed English travel writer, Fynes Moryson (1566–1630), noted his observations after a visit to the Netherlands in 1592: 'And the cold is so extreme in these parts, as most part of [the] winter these ditches of water are continually frozen... and upon the broadest waters [people] slide together upon the ice. To which purpose they put upon their shoes pattens of wood, with a long sharp iron in the bottom to cut the ice.' In the Netherlands, in contrast to other countries, you may skate almost anywhere out-of-doors. This was necessary long ago, because goods as well as people were transported by means of water (in the summer) and ice (in the winter). The Dutch heir to the throne, Willem-Alexander, even proposed marriage to Máxima on the ice. If you go skating on natural ice, not only will you meet the Dutch in a relaxed setting, but you will get to know this beautiful country at its best.

Doing business in the Netherlands and/or with the Dutch

Business relations, talks and negotiations with the Dutch generally proceed smoothly here. But there might be some things that are done differently. Remember the Dutch attach importance to planning and using time efficiently. This means:

1. Be punctual, that is to say: neither early nor late. Someone who arrives late runs the risk of being perceived as unreliable. If you have an appointment in a large office complex, arrive five to ten minutes early. Then you have the time to locate where you are going, to walk the stairs, take the lift and navigate the long corridors so you won't be late.
2. Ring up if you are going to be delayed.
3. Don't wear out your welcome: don't use more time than necessary to arrange your affairs.
4. Do not sit down until you are invited to.
5. Try to avoid cancelling appointments at the last minute. These are usually precisely scheduled and therefore difficult to change on short notice.

For this reason:

6. Never show up unannounced.

'Drinking coffee together is essential for the
scientific and cultural exchange in the Netherlands.'
(Setiyo Hadi Waluyo, Wageningen University, 2000)

❖❖

In the land of meetings, meetings and more meetings

Talking, talking, talking and compromising – so-called *polderen* – to reach a consensus. Why is it that the Dutch spend endless amounts of time in meetings, sometimes to the utter despair of foreigners? And add to this the notions of *inspraak* (having a say in a matter) and *medezeggenschap* (having even more of a say), which can further delay and even thwart the decision-making process. A good example of this is found in the revealing documentary *The New Rijksmuseum* (2008) by Dutch filmmaker Oeke Hoogendijks (2008). Amsterdam's world-famous museum was supposed to close for two years to be renovated, but the completion of this project has now been delayed by many years. This is primarily because of the opposition exerted by: *welstandscommissies* (committees commissioned by a municipal government to evaluate the aesthetic aspects of a building plan) and *stadsdelen* (the city boroughs); cyclists (who want to continue riding underneath the building's main passageway); the rest of the population of Amsterdam, which is also allowed their say. More than eighty licences were required! This film follows the endless discussions of all parties involved. When the umpteenth licence is not issued, the Spanish architect almost explodes in frustration: 'I'm fed up with all these difficulties', he exclaims. 'In this kind of process nobody is prepared to take risks. This is too Dutch for me...'

All of this endless discussion basically stems from the unusual form of government that existed in the *Republiek der*

Zeven Verenigde Provinciën (Republic of the Seven United Provinces), established in 1588 and recognised in 1648 as an independent state. It was a fairly loose confederation, a kind of European Union or United Arab Emirates ahead of its time, with far-reaching autonomy for the provinces.

Each province had its own governing board, called the *Provinciale Staten*. And the cities within these provinces, certainly the somewhat larger ones, also enjoyed a relative degree of self-rule. Regarding the nobility: they had to hand over their leadership positions to wealthy and influential merchants early on. The communal affairs (foreign policy, defence, finances, etc.) of the individual *Provinciale Staten* were regulated in the so-called *Staten-Generaal* (forerunner of the Dutch Parliament). This met in The Hague; each province sent its own representatives to this governing body. Therefore, a single ruler could not impose his decisions from above. Consequently, the government here did not function top-down, as was the case in many kingdoms, but bottom-up. Of course there were the Princes of Orange, but they were *stadhouders* (stadtholders: governors or viceroys) and therefore servants of the *Staten*. They were surely not heads of state, even if they behaved as princely as possible at certain moments.

That is how we ended up with our Dutch way of conducting meetings. It certainly isn't surprising that this decentralisation of power made the decision-making process at the meetings of the *Staten-Generaal* lengthy and difficult. For almost every decision that had to be taken in The Hague, the representative first had to return to their province to consult at a lower level. Only then could they return to the higher level of the *Staten-Generaal*. This so-called *last en ruggespraak* (instruction and consultation) took time, lots of time.

Furthermore, the representatives had to weigh the pros and cons of national versus provincial interests, which could often conflict. And then add that to this the power and influence exerted by the leading factions did not differ significantly. All this resulted in meetings being painstaking and drawn out and led to compromises having to be reached.

This pluralist approach also continued into the 19th century. And this is how talking, talking, talking became second nature to the Dutch.

❖❖

Some other characteristics of the Dutch:
- Hierarchy is of little account (*primus inter pares*, 'first among equals'): the team comes before the individual. This means that also trainees and younger employees actively participate at meetings.
- They shake hands before and after meetings.
- They quickly get personal. At the office they happily talk about private matters such as their house, children, dog(s), holidays, etc. After all, *gezelligheid* (that 'group hug' feeling) is a must! But let me warn you again: do not see this informal behaviour as a sign of friendship (see also p. 56).

- ❖ Humour and jokes are appreciated.
- ❖ They are not upset by directness: straightforward opinions and critical observations are the order of the day. When the Dutch don't agree with you, they don't beat around the bush but come right out and say it: *Nee hoor, dat vind ik helemaal niet.* (No, I absolutely disagree.) Do not confuse this directness with rudeness.
- ❖ They may ask questions or offer commentary completely out of the blue. One expat related: 'Granted my infant son is somewhat chubby, but when I have gone out for walks with him, I have gotten unsolicited comments like he must have eaten everything but the kitchen sink, or wow, a baby Michelin Man.'
- ❖ They seldom use the words please, sorry and thank you.
- ❖ Talk, talk, talk: the Dutch are constantly busy with *overleggen* (deliberating). Their so-called *polder*-model (slowly working towards a consensus or compromise) is all about influence because one strives, as they say in Dutch: *de neuzen van alle betrokkenen dezelfde kant op te laten wijzen* (literally to get the noses of everybody involved pointed in the same direction). But this also leads to getting bogged down in endless discussion sessions (including *inspraak*, 'having a say') and this is not always productive. Foreigners sometimes long for a person of authority to simply take the lead and make the decision. Another disadvantage of this democratic approach is that nobody feels responsible.
- ❖ They prefer a brisk, personal presentation without being bogged down in stacks of papers.

- They are flexible: prefer not to set everything in stone. *De rest komt wel!* (We'll get to it later!) or *'t Komt wel goed!* (It'll be fine!) is more their attitude. Advantage: they can quickly react to problems when these arise. Disadvantage: in a complicated situation, they sometimes take no responsibility and hide behind: *Dat zijn nu eenmaal de regels* (Rules are rules) (also see p. 118).

- They prefer dealing with disputes personally (via the telephone or with a visit) to relying on lawyers.

- At the beginning of a brief business meeting, your Dutch business partner might be busy with another matter; may not have the dossier you want to discuss readily available; could have you wait for a few minutes and might even ask preoccupied: *Wat was ook weer de bedoeling?* (What were we going to discuss again?) This is not meant discourteously. The other person simply wants to finish up something else and assumes you don't mind.

- Office hours may differ from other countries. Take into account that lots of Dutch people still like to eat dinner around 6 p.m. and therefore head home from work relatively early.

And finally do not forget their aversion to *poeha* (hoo ha or fuss). Keep in mind those well-known Dutch sayings, also mentioned earlier on: *Doe maar gewoon* (Be normal) and *Nooit met je kop boven het maaiveld uitsteken* (Never let your head rise above the parapet). Consequently don't be too conspicuous; keep your head down... otherwise it might get chopped off! This means as a businessman or businesswoman:

- Do not be tempted into showing off your wealth and status. Better to avoid arriving at a meeting in a flashy car or striking designer suit. And don't come bearing expensive business gifts – nor expect to receive them.

- Demonstrate modesty. Therefore, avoid endless and long-winded statements when doing a presentation or introducing your new product; keep it short and businesslike. Also do not boast too much. Don't exclaim: 'We're the best and brightest', because you will be perceived as a braggart. Remember 'time is money', and the Dutch have a reputation for being frugal.

- Be honest. The Dutch value integrity and score high in this area. So do not expect personal favours for a business transaction (and certainly don't ask for any).

- Jackets and ties (depending on the type of business or company) could be removed right away. And at times the Dutch quickly switch to addressing people by their first names or with *je* or *jij* (the informal forms of you or yours). However, it is best to let your Dutch host(s) take the lead in this respect.

- Titles (professional or academic) are not used.

- The usual office lunch in the Netherlands is short (approximately forty-five minutes), cold and simple: sandwiches with ham or cheese, currant (raisin) buns, milk, buttermilk, coffee, for dessert yogurt or a fruit. There are people who complain about this: 'How is it possible that I can't get a warm lunch in the company canteen?' they wonder, often a bit irritated. Or: 'In other countries there's a real lunch pause. In the Netherlands, it isn't at all unusual to keep meeting while you're eating. Maddening!' Indeed...this is the Dutch way, restrained and *gewoon* (normal). So: when in Rome do as the Romans do.

And last but not least, two well-loved Dutch traditions:

Kerstpakketten (Christmas boxes or hampers): Once a year, in the days leading up to Christmas, many Dutch companies and organisations give each of their employees a so-called *kerstpakket*. Such gift boxes usually contain food and (alcoholic) beverages as well as practical luxury products, anything from a suitcase on wheels to a hand blender.

Verjaardagen (birthdays): Celebrating one's birthday is frightfully important to the Dutch and also happens at the workplace. It is normal at most companies and organisations for the *feestvarken* (literally party pig, meaning the person celebrating his or her birthday) to bring in a cake or something else delicious for the morning coffee break. And as an expat you are not exempt. As the centre of attention, you have the honour of cutting your cake and handing out pieces to all your colleagues. The coffee and cake are meant to be consumed with everybody relaxing and chatting together.

Writing: (Formal) letters and e-mails

It is wise to be particularly attentive when sending letters and e-mails. As you are a foreigner, you need to take cultural sensitivities that could arise into account. When you communicate by post or via the Internet, body language, facial expressions and voice intonations do not play a role. Therefore, misunderstandings can easily occur. Play it safe and carefully compose your letters and/or e-mails.

A few fine points

On the whole: Be careful! Make sure your e-mails and letters are formal, businesslike and grammatically correct. If you are writing to a specific person make sure that his or her entire name and any eventual title(s) are correct, even if you normally address each other by your first names.

Salutations: You might receive a mass mailing or an impersonal letter in Dutch that begins with *LS*. This is Latin and stands for *Lectori salutem* which means 'Greetings to the reader'. The equivalent in English is usually: 'To whom it may concern'. Among themselves, academics, politicians and professionals (lawyers, doctors, etc.) in the Netherlands use the salutation *Amice* or *Amica* (friend).

Confirmations: Always confirm the receipt of important messages.

Introductions: Do you need to request something from your Dutch colleagues or subordinates by e-mail or letter? Then be careful about being too blunt and first briefly introduce the matter. Remember: the Dutch do not like being issued commands! They like to be informed and prefer to be asked to do things in a friendly manner. According to some expats it's more like 'you have to beg them on your hands and knees to get something done, because, yes – you mustn't think you're better than the next guy...'

As an example, a British expat from a large company shot off the following e-mail to her Dutch subordinates:

'Hello all,

Could you please complete this budget spreadsheet by 2 p.m. tomorrow, because I need it for a meeting with the boss.

Kind regards,

...'

To her surprise, the Dutch were rather offended – they were not going to be ordered about. She could have better formulated it as:

'Dear all,

I have a meeting tomorrow afternoon with... about the budget of... So could you please complete this budget spreadsheet, so I will have the correct information? I would be most grateful if you could get this to me by 2 p.m. tomorrow at the latest.

Kind regards,

...'

E-mail a bit less. There is much too much e-mailing going on nowadays. This can lead to misunderstandings and even irritations. And what's more: it is rather impersonal. So pick up the telephone more often instead of endlessly mailing back-and-forth. It is often quicker and easier to make appointments verbally than via e-mail. You can also qualify things, speak in a reassuring tone and provide more information.

And get up from your desk and go over to your (Dutch) colleagues on the work floor more often. This is helpful for maintaining good contact.

Business cards: These are useful for having the correct names, titles and functions of your business relations at your disposal. Some frequently occurring academic titles: *dr.* (doctor) = PhD (American doctorate) or DPhil (British doctorate); *drs.* from the word *doctorandus* in Latin = a university graduate with a Master's degree in Arts or Science; *ir.* = engineer (with a degree from a Technical University); *mr.* (Dutch Master of Laws degree) = lawyer.

❖❖

High and Mightiness

In the Netherlands – although you think it's the land of equality – elaborate forms of address have been used here since way back. This basically stems from the fact that our country was a republic for a long time. The citizens were the ones who made the decisions not the aristocrats, which was the case in the monarchies surrounding the Netherlands. But, as a republic, our country could not bestow noble titles. Therefore so-called *burgerlijke* (civilian) titles were invented, each one more beautiful than the next. The members of the *Staten-Generaal* chose to be addressed as *Hoogmogende Heren* (Highly Wealthy Gentlemen). Of course there were no ladies among them. The Governor-General of the Dutch East Indies Company (VOC) was addressed as *Hoog Edelheid* (Your Noble Honour), members of the Dutch Board of Admiralty were *Hoogedelgestrenge Heren* (High and Mighty Gentlemen), while the Stadtholder – the Prince of Orange – was only addressed as *Excellentie* (Your Excellency). But in 1639, the King of France was so friendly as to allow Frederick Henry, Prince of Orange, to be addressed as *Hoogheid* (*Altesse* in French or Highness).

All in all, it was a sophisticated system of titles such as *Edelgrootachtbare*, *Hoogwelgeboren* and *Weledelgestrenge Heren en Vrouwen*, 'High and Mighty, Highly noble and well-bred, Wealthy and mighty Gentlemen' that are only still used today in very formal correspondence, for instance by the Dutch Royal House.

✿✿✿

Trouble communicating

Expatriates complain about communicating with Dutch people in three particular areas: contact with doctors; with agencies and organisations; with the personnel in restaurants, shops etc. More details related to these top three areas of irritation follow here:

1. Dutch health care: 'No bedside manners!'

Nearly all surveys indicate that expatriates do not trust the Dutch health care system. The major criticism being that it fails to meet their desires. A few examples:

- ❖ 'Doctors have no bedside manners; they are very Dutch, i.e. very direct, not accustomed to using gentle words. They are not trained to be empathetic, concerned, caring.'
- ❖ 'In other countries you're treated more like a client than a patient.'
- ❖ 'There is a reluctance to prescribe antibiotics and painkillers. But in other countries, people are simply given this kind of medication. Here they say: "Go home, take some paracetamol, get some rest". It's as if the doctor is not willing to help you. But we, expats, want pills!'

As an expat, you will probably have to get accustomed to the Dutch approach. With non-urgent physical or mental medical problems – just like the Dutch – you are first expected to consult your neighbourhood *huisarts* (family doctor or GP). Then only if he or she deems it necessary you will be referred to a specialist or a hospital. The average appointment with a Dutch GP lasts ten minutes.

In the meantime, something is finally being done about complaints such as these that mainly result because of the cultural differences between the Dutch and expats (see p. 23).

There is however, one Dutch custom you can easily adopt: always greet the people in the doctor's waiting room with a friendly *Goedendag* (Good day or Hello). It's also very Dutch if you then inquire who was the last to arrive, because that person has their turn right before you. By the way, this polite practice also applies in shops, at information desks, etc.

2. Dutch bureaucracy: 'Rules are rules!'

As already mentioned, the Dutch are mad about equality and the notion of *polderen* (working towards a compromise). In this way, they avoid as many conflicts as possible. But there are also disadvantages: this has led to a dense web of procedures and instructions. Foreigners, in particular, often find themselves tangled up in this. 'The Dutch were portrayed to me as easy-going and informal', said a Swede. 'But they love procedures and now and then can be frustratingly bureaucratic. I couldn't believe I had to wait four weeks for an Internet connection.' Another expat needed tons of forms from the Dutch customs in order to get her things shipped from New Zealand to the Netherlands.

'They don't think ahead or go out of their way to help you,' is also a complaint you will hear. An American: 'You have to fill out all these forms; you have finally done it and hand them in, then the man says: "You forgot the blue form!" So I reply: "But I don't have a blue form, why didn't you give me one?" "You didn't ask me for one..." the man replies. So then you can get back in line all over again! And if you get aggravated, the response is invariably: "Rules are rules!"'

3. Dutch (lack of) service: 'I don't know and even if I did...'

'I'm sorry to have to say it,' one expat remarked, 'but the service personnel in stores, restaurants and the like come across as rude and unhelpful. When you ask someone something you frequently get an annoyed response such as "I don't know", or "We don't have it", "No, we can't do that" or "That's not possible".' Most expatriates agree on this and say they don't experience the Dutch as customer-friendly. They add to this that service people actually seem rather skilled at avoiding eye contact, particularly in cafés and restaurants. 'You would almost think they study this avoidance technique at *Horeca* (*Ho*tel, *re*staurant, *ca*tering) school,' another expat chimed in.

By now these top-three irritations have also come to the attention of the Dutch government, businesses and hospitals. For this reason, so-called expat centres have been established in several large Dutch cities. Here expatriates receive a warm welcome and are helped with any issues that might arise. Certain companies, too, have their own expat desk.

The purple crocodile

Even the Dutch themselves are not immune to the exaggerated Dutch bureaucracy. You will sometimes hear them refer to a Dutch television commercial about a purple crocodile, which has come to exemplify this problem. It depicts a mother asking the man in the ticket-seller's booth of a swimming pool if the inflatable purple crocodile belonging to her young daughter has, by any chance, been found. Though the crocodile is propped in a corner directly behind him, the man responds in rather a blasé tone that the mother needs to fill in a certain form. 'But it's right there', she says. He's not impressed and tells her she also needs to complete the reverse side. Once she's done that, he pushes the entire form back in her direction instructing: 'File tomorrow morning between 9 a.m. and 10 a.m. with the Recreation Department.' The woman repeats in an exasperated tone: 'But it's right there, behind you!' The man agrees: 'Yes, it's right there', but to her despair he doesn't do anything else to help her.

5

VISITING THE DUTCH

Ja, gezellig! [gggg-zell-lig], 'Oh, how cosy!'

The Dutch thrive on *gezelligheid* (cosiness) and use the word *gezellig* constantly. Generally speaking, it means a warm and fuzzy feeling, a togetherness that knows no bounds. A *gezellig* atmosphere is one that allows good times to happen. It is almost like a vibe. And it is contagious. That is why the Dutch enjoy inviting people over to their homes: *Kom je op mijn verjaardag?*, 'Think you can make it to my birthday? Ja, gezellig!'

There are all kinds of occasions for visiting the Dutch at home. Many are included in this chapter. Except, it does not happen just like that...so what better way to begin than with the *agenda* (datebook).

THE ALL-IMPORTANT *agenda*

I've already mentioned a few times that the Dutch are orderly and fond of planning ahead. So it is advisable not to show up on a Dutch person's doorstep unannounced, since the Dutch tend not to appreciate this. They regard unexpected guests as unsettling, because:

- ❖ They have not been able to prepare!
- ❖ They are too busy!

- They have another appointment!
- They have not had a chance to tidy up their house!
- And if you happen to show up unexpectedly, the Dutch will almost always excuse themselves by saying: 'Please, don't mind the mess. I wasn't expecting anybody.'

Nonetheless, this can also go differently as a Romanian girl living in the Netherlands experienced: 'Close Dutch friends repeatedly told me: "You must come round for dinner." One day I went and rang their doorbell, looking forward to a nice evening. My friend opened the door and said: "It is 6 o'clock, we are having dinner." "Oh splendid," I said, thinking this to be an excellent opportunity to join them. But my friend did not let me in. She was blocking the doorway and repeated: "We are having dinner." I still did not get it and said: "Oh, *gezellig*." Only after her third "We are having dinner" I understood what was going on: I was definitely not welcome. I cannot tell you how deeply disappointed I was.'

What should you do then if you want to visit someone (even if it's only the neighbour)? You need to make an official appointment beforehand, even for a cup of coffee. That is how it's done here: telephone first, check your *agenda* and set a specific date and time. Only then, when it has been jotted down in the unavoidable *agenda*, do you actually have an appointment.

Many expats see this as just another one of those incomprehensible Dutch formalities. 'What a regimented social life! You can't even invite the average Dutch person for drinks that same day, but need to book them a month or two in advance', one expat sighed. A Spaniard related: 'In Spain, friends can always drop in without announcing their arrival beforehand, even during meals, whereas in the Netherlands an appointment has to be made at least a fortnight in advance.'

Meanwhile, some expats have grown accustomed to this use of datebooks. Listen to what the Greek expat Vasilios said: 'When I was in Greece during my last holiday I asked my brother: "What are we going to do the weekend after next?" My brother couldn't believe his ears. He looked at me in astonishment and said: "You must be joking. I don't even know what we are doing this afternoon."'

EATING AND DRINKING: DIVIDING UP THE DUTCH DAY

Before going into more detail about the different kinds of visits possible in the Netherlands, first something about the eating and drinking habits of the average Dutch person.

1. *Ontbijt* (breakfast): Consists of slices of bread (white, brown, whole wheat) with margarine (sometimes butter) and a variety of (sandwich) fillings: cheese of course, sometimes an egg, but also meat products such as the traditional Dutch *rookvlees* (thinly sliced smoked beef), peanut butter, *appelstroop* (apple spread resembling a thick pancake syrup), *hagelslag* (usually chocolate sprinkles, but also available in other flavours), *ge-*

Broodje kroket (see p. 143)

stampte muisjes (a crumble of sugared aniseed), etc. These are foods all Dutch people grow up eating and willingly take along with them if they themselves become expats. On the breakfast table you may also find: *krentenbollen* (currant buns), *ontbijt-koek* (kind of spicy gingerbread cake), yogurt, muesli, etc. The Dutch drink tea, coffee and/or milk, buttermilk and orange juice for breakfast.

2. *Koffietijd* (literally coffee time, also coffee break): Between 10 a.m. and 12 noon, the Dutch drink coffee (with or without sugar and *koffiemelk,* a sort of condensed milk), accompanied by a sweet biscuit.

3. *Middageten, koffietafel* or *twaalfuurtje* (different Dutch words re-ferring to lunch): Between 12 noon and 2 p.m., the Dutch gener-ally eat the same foods they ate for breakfast. They also enjoy a typical Dutch snack called a *kroket* (a deep-fried croquette or rissole, with a creamy meat or shrimp filling) – also often eaten on a soft bun or a slice of white bread.

4. *Thee* (tea): From around 3 p.m. until approximately 4.30 p.m., the Dutch drink tea also with a sweet biscuit.

5. *Borrel* (aperitif): Between 5 p.m. and 7 p.m. is generally the time to unwind with a drink. Traditionally, the Dutch drink a *borreltje* (a *jenever*: pungent juniper-flavoured gin) or a beer, wine, sher-ry, or another (non-)alcoholic drink. This is accompanied by so-called *borrelhapjes* (snacks) such as cheese, pieces of sausage, savoury snacks, peanuts, crisps and of course those famous Dutch *bitterballen (*smaller, rounder versions of the Dutch cro-

quette eaten as appetizers) usually served with mustard.

6. *Avondeten* (dinner): Takes place between 6 p.m. and 8 p.m., but nowadays many Dutch people still eat promptly at 6 p.m.

7. *Na het eten* (after dinner): A cup of coffee or tea and possibly a glass of wine or another alcoholic beverage later in the evening. Be careful you don't find yourself in the same situation as one German expat: she was invited over to a Dutch person's home at 8 p.m. To her amazement, she was only offered a cup of coffee...except she had not eaten yet!

❖❖

There is always time for coffee

The cultural significance of the sacred coffee break for the Dutch is not something you run across in other countries. It dates back to the 18th century, when coffee and tea became popular as new and exotic drinks. These beverages quickly became established in the Netherlands as part of snacking between meals, which included something sweet to eat. The present-day afternoon cups of tea and particularly that holy cup of coffee in the morning with a sweet biscuit are remnants of this. At the office, a person's home – no matter where you might be between 10 a.m. and 12 noon, there must and there will be coffee to drink, otherwise the Dutch cannot function. No less than seventy percent of coffee in the Netherlands is consumed at home and around thirty percent outside the door. This percentage is exactly the opposite in southern European countries. As an expat, this means for instance if painters or repairmen are working in your home, you are expected to offer them coffee – accompanied by a sweet biscuit of course.

So it should not surprise you that it is quite common in the Netherlands to invite someone for coffee, or as the Dutch say: *op de koffie vragen*. Dutch women gladly organise *koffieochtenden* (coffee mornings) for other women. Simply for the *gezelligheid* (cosiness), to see the neighbours or to celebrate a birthday.

Oh, you have been invited for coffee? Then don't be surprised either if your visit goes according to the oh-so special coffee etiquette: everything is ready when you arrive, your hostess pours a first cup of coffee, hands this over and offers you a biscuit or another (sweet) delicacy. After some time the second round follows: another cup of coffee including another biscuit. Then you are supposed to go home.

Important: always wait to be served! The Dutch consider it impolite if you serve yourself. Also keep this in mind when you receive Dutch people at home. Offer them coffee, tea, wine, biscuits or whatever because they will be reluctant to help themselves, even if you emphatically say: 'Please, help yourselves!' To illustrate: a Dutch couple was visiting a Swedish couple. There was a smorgasbord of all kinds of delicious things to eat, but the Dutch people didn't touch anything because their hosts had not offered them something to start.

The important role that coffee plays in the Netherlands also accounts for Dutch expressions such as *dat is geen zuivere koffie* (literally that coffee isn't pure, meaning something is a bit suspicious), *op de koffie komen* (meaning being conned or cheated) and *zullen we daar een kop koffie op drinken?* (literally shall we drink a cup of coffee to that?, as a way of making up or settling something). But the Frisians say: *Foar de koffie net eamelje!* (No moaning before coffee!)

❖❖❖

THE DUTCH HOME FRONT

Typisch Nederlands!, 'Typically Dutch!'

You could get invited to a Dutch person's home for various reasons: the well-loved cup of coffee, lunch, afternoon tea, a drink (from 5 p.m. on), dinner, coffee/tea (8 p.m.) or ultimately a glass of wine or other (alcoholic) beverage later in the evening.

Some helpful tips:

❖ Be punctual. For a 10.30 a.m. appointment you should arrive between 10.30 a.m. and 10.45 a.m. not later, but certainly not earlier (because then your host or hostess will not be ready yet and you might upset his or her planning).

❖ Greet everybody when you arrive: shake hands with everyone in the room (also with any children), unless, for instance, there are more than twenty people present. If you are not introduced, then introduce yourself with your (first and) last name.

❖ Do not sit down unless you are invited to.

❖ After drinking a cup of coffee or tea do not rest your spoon across the top of the cup, but place it alongside the cup in the saucer.

❖ It is considered polite to always empty your cup (tea, coffee), contrary for instance to Arab countries where this is perceived as unmannerly. In these countries an empty cup or glass is considered a lack of hospitality.

Table manners

❖ Before eating, there may be a request for *een ogenblik stilte* (a moment of silence) for those who want to offer thanks in the form of a prayer.

❖ Always wait to be served, unless you are explicitly instructed to help yourself. At a buffet sandwich lunch, after you have been served the first sandwich, you will probably be encouraged to help yourself.

❖ Never start eating before the host or hostess. Once he or she has taken their first bite, that is the sign for guests to start eating.

❖ Also do not begin drinking just like that, but wait until everyone raises their glass in a toast. Only afterwards may you drink. An Englishman who was not aware of this was at an important business lunch and took a sip of his wine as soon as the waiter had poured it: 'It simply did not occur to me. We had already

had a drink beforehand. But I realised soon enough that this was a *faux pas* (indiscretion). The Dutch always begin with a toast and then drink together. I still remember how embarrassed I felt.'

- Place both your hands on the table during meals. Do not rest your left hand in your lap or under the table, which is the custom in some countries. This difference in table manners can be historically explained. Long ago, people used their knife and fork one after the other: they first cut their meat into bite-size pieces, put down their knife, picked up their fork with their right hand and then brought these pieces to their mouth. Around 1900, the custom arose of using these utensils together: fork in the left hand and knife in the right hand. This way of using utensils is completely established in the Netherlands. 'Keep your hands on top of the table during meals!' remains an important rule.
- Conversation is important. But do not inquire about someone's salary, mortgage or other personal money matters – this is not done!
- Don't go to the lavatory during dinner. Do this in advance.
- Special objects that you might find on a Dutch table include: the *kaasschaaf* (cheese slicer to cut cheese as thinly as possible) and the *flessenschraper* or *flessenlikker* (literally a bottle scraper or licker), a long thin rubber or plastic object with a half circle at the end designed to scrap the last bits of mayonnaise, salad dressing etc. There is an amusing story about a Papal slicer. In

honour of Pope John Paul II visiting the Netherlands in 1985, he was given a cheese slicer. While other countries gave him sparkling chalices or other ceremonial silver objects, the Netherlands chose for a novel keepsake – the trusted Dutch *kaasschaaf*.

Lastly, many foreigners mentioned one Dutch practice that they find particularly charming: 'The Dutch have such a nice way of bidding goodbye to visitors. When you are leaving, they keep waving outside on the street until they can no longer see you.'

❖❖

Cadeautjes: The importance of giving

When you visit people at home in the Netherlands, it is common practice to bring a small present. This is meant as a kind gesture, nothing more and nothing less and could consist of: a bundle of flowers, something delicious to eat like chocolates, a bottle of wine, sweet-smelling soap, a candle, a book, some kind of a gift certificate, etc. Your present will be even more personal or memorable if you take the time to beautifully wrap it yourself.

Giving such a *cadeautje* (*tje* = small) is odd for some expats: in their country, a small present says something about the status of the giver as well as the receiver. The Argentinian Graciela

Prosperi related: 'In Argentina abundance and generosity are demonstrated by giving presents. You are supposed to make an impression with your present and show that you have carefully chosen it especially for that person and the occasion.'

An Englishman had another experience. When he was invited to eat at the home of his Dutch boss, a colleague recommended that he bring flowers for his boss's wife. But he thought it was absurd: 'How can I justify giving flowers to someone I have never even met?' So he did not do this, but now he knows better.

However, important to note is that I am referring to personal visits here. This means if you, for instance, are invited to eat with a member of the Royal Family, or with an ambassador, that you do not have to bring anything along, not even flowers. These dinners are given within the framework of their work. But if you are invited because you're a good friend, then of course you can bring something with you.

And finally remember: the Dutch always immediately unpack a present so they can express their thanks. If the receiver does not like it, or has it already, then he or she should refrain from indicating this, because to say so would be unkind and therefore impolite.

Finally, I cannot emphasise enough that if you don't know what to expect at a Dutch person's home, simply ask. Do not be embarrassed to say that you are new here, that you are a foreigner, and to ask what you should wear and what time you should arrive. And when it comes to giving a present you can always consult other people you know who are also invited.

The importance of asking for more details is illustrated by the fact that I have met expats who are afraid to accept any invitations, basically because they are unfamiliar with how the Dutch do things. For example, when invited to a birthday party on a Sunday between 3 p.m. and 8 p.m. they are generally uncertain about questions such as:

⋄ When should they arrive?
⋄ How long should they stay?
⋄ What should they wear?
⋄ Should they bring a present? And if so, what? Should it be large or small?
⋄ What will be served? Tea? Hors d'oeuvres and drinks? An entire meal?

And so on and so forth.

You are what you eat
Traditionally, food from the Dutch kitchen has always been simple, heavy and hearty. In earlier centuries, foreigners were amazed about this...as well as by the lack of decorum at the dining table. A German visitor in the 18th century complained about the food (too

much fish and heavy *stamppotten*, 'stews with mashed potatoes') and the lack of table manners: 'The Dutch burp and fart at the table and – oh, disgraceful – don't even remove their hats!' Other foreigners expressed similar sentiments. They were also struck by the Dutch habit of eating largely to fill their bellies and the way they gulped the meal down. Enjoyment didn't seem to be involved. Later, in the 19th century, a Portuguese visitor described how Dutch business people in restaurants took a seat, tucked their napkins into the front of their shirts, spread out their papers on the table and ate while they were calculating sums or arranging their notes.

And what do the Dutch enjoy eating and drinking nowadays? A few examples:

Broodje kaas **(cheese sandwich):** It's not for nothing that the Dutch are called *kaaskoppen* (cheeseheads). There is always room for a cheese sandwich. It's traditional fare in this dairy-rich country both for breakfast and lunch. Already at the beginning of the 17th century, Dutch artists such as Floris van Dijck painted still lives portraying bread, cheese and fruit – appropriately entitled *ontbijtjes* (breakfast pieces). Foreigners have always been astounded by this. In those days, they related, there was nothing more normal than seeing the average citizen sitting outside by his front door eating a piece of bread with butter and cheese. And the Spanish ambassador was horror-stricken when around 1660 he encountered members of the *Staten-Generaal* (forerunner Dutch Parliament) on the main square (Lange Voorhout) in The Hague sitting on benches, eating bread and cheese with their hands. That such *Hoge Heren* (important gentlemen) were eating outside on the street was incomprehensible for the Spaniard.

Borrel (shot of liquor): This all-important drink for the Dutch was already customary in the *Gouden Eeuw* (Dutch Golden Age roughly spanning the 17th century) as this short verse from 1685 about drinking beer illustrates.

> *Het eerste is een glaasje voor de gezondheid.*
> *Het tweede voor de smaak.*
> *Het derde is een slaapdrank.*
> *De rest kan niet dienen tot vermaak.*

> The first is a glass for your health.
> The second is for the fine taste.
> The third is a sleeping potion.
> The rest is merely a waste.

Between these glasses of beer, the Dutch drank *jenever* (juniper-flavoured gin); this was (and still is) called a *borrel*. People had a preference for referring to it as a *borreltje* (little drink) and still do – to emphasise the diminutive, invoke something that is innocent or harmless and, of course, *gezellig* (cosy).

Borrel, in the sense of 'a little something to drink', is a Dutch word that goes way back. It was apparently first used in an Amsterdam theatrical comedy in 1685. That was the beginning of people seeing signs hanging on taverns with texts such as *Hier gaat de borrel, dag en nacht!* (Drinking around the clock!) and *Hier tapt men borrel, uit den treure* (Here, we never stop pouring).

Another special custom in those days was loudly reciting *gelegenheidsgedichten* or *liederen* (poems or songs for special occasions) at social gatherings, festive meals, receptions, etc. Even today, the Dutch continue to enjoy reciting and singing verses they have composed for special occasions such as marriages, anniversaries, *Sinterklaas* (the yearly St. Nicholas celebration).

Stamppot (hodgepodge, hotchpotch, mishmash or simply stew in combination with potatoes mashed with one or several other vegetables): One of the most frequently-eaten foods in the Netherlands, going as far back as the Middle Ages, is a warm dish that was then referred to as *potspijs* or *hutspot* – the one-pot meal. This became very popular due to the limitations of cooking on one open fire long ago. Therefore Dutch housewives cooked one-pot meals on such a fire in a cauldron. Today the Dutch are still fond of eating dishes such as these, especially in the winter.

Margarine: The Dutch eat all kinds of things on bread. But one thing is a bit odd. In this land with an abundance of dairy products, the Dutch often do not spread their bread with butter, but with

margarine – which is made from vegetable oils. They were initially suspicious of this artificial butter developed in 1869 by the French because they were unsure about how it was made. But the Dutch were forced to use margarine during World War II and the few years thereafter due to shortages. And so they became accustomed to margarine, so much so that nowhere else in Europe is so much margarine and so little butter used as in the Netherlands. Perhaps a helpful tip: the Dutch refer to real butter as *roomboter* and to margarine as *boter*.

Here is a more detailed list of typically Dutch foods eaten nowadays. Hopefully, you will have a chance to try them all.

* Dutch one-pot meals: *Boerenkoolstamppot* (mash with kale), *zuurkoolstamppot* (mash with sauerkraut), *hete bliksem* (mash with apples and onions), *hutspot* (mash with carrots and onions) and *erwtensoep* (pea soup) – also called *snert* – with pieces of *rookworst* (smoked sausage).
* *Pannekoeken* (pancakes): Eaten as a main course, generally with bacon and *stroop* (treacle or molasses).
* *Haring* (herring): Salted but raw and accompanied by diced onions and/or pickles (the classic Dutch delicacy – grasp it by the tail, hold it above your mouth as you tilt your head back and slowly let it slither between your teeth as you continue chewing).
* Indonesian *rijsttafel* (literally rice table): This meal harks back to the Dutch colonial past in *Nederlands-Indië* (now Indonesia)

and consists of all sorts of different chicken, pork and beef dishes as well as eggs, warm and cold vegetables, *loempia's* (spring rolls), *kroepoek* (shrimp crackers), noodles or rice and whatever else people might add. Everything is placed on the table at the same time and everyone helps themselves to whatever they want to eat.

* *Uitsmijter* (for breakfast or lunch): Two fried eggs with ham or cheese served on slices of bread.
* *Broodje kroket* (deep-fried croquette or risolle on a soft roll) or *broodje frikandel* (deep-fried minced-meat hot dog on a soft roll): The Dutch love grabbing one of these *uit de muur* (literally from the wall), meaning snack automats.
* *Chocoladeletter* (large chocolate letter), *pepernoten* (bite-sized round gingerbread cookies), *banketstaaf* (almond-filled pastry roll), *kikkers and muizen* (literally frogs and mice made from sugary fondant or even chocolate): Traditional treats eaten especially during the period when *Sinterklaas* (St. Nicholas) visits the Netherlands (mid-November through 6 December).
* *Oliebollen* (deep-fried dough balls): Covered with powder sugar, traditionally eaten on *Oudejaarsavond* (New Year's Eve).

Birthdays

Verjaardagen (birthdays) are a category all onto themselves because of how important they are to the Dutch. In order not to forget when someone celebrates their birthday, nearly every Dutch person has a so-called *verjaardagskalender* (birthday calendar) hanging in

their lavatory. All birthdays of people near and dear are noted there. It is common practice on birthdays to visit people at home, to send a card/e-mail with congratulations, or to personally ring someone on the telephone.

The Dutch are fond of inviting all sorts of people to their birthday: family and close friends of course, but also acquaintances, neighbours and often colleagues from work. Have you been invited to such a party? Then make sure to check on the details in advance: what time are you expected to arrive, is it with or without food (after 8 p.m. you will probably not be fed), what kind of clothing should you wear, what present would the person whose birthday it is enjoy (or perhaps a group gift has been arranged, for which someone is collecting money), etc. Knowing all this will spare you lots of uncertainty. Please note: make sure your present is not too expensive. This could easily embarrass a Dutch person. Many people throw a sort of 'open house' for their birthday, meaning that people can come and go as they please within a certain time frame.

Distinctive about the Dutch birthday party is the custom of congratulating not only the person celebrating their birthday, but also their parents, children, neighbours etc. This funny custom probably stems from the Dutch obsession with equality: if one person is celebrating their birthday, then somehow it is a little bit everybody else's birthday too.

The room is usually decorated with party streamers. Of course all those in attendance take part in singing the (Dutch) 'Happy birthday' song *Lang zal hij* (or *ze*) *leven!* (wishing someone a long life), which is sometimes followed by the congratulatory tune *Hij* (or *Zij*) *leve hoog!* (wishing that person a good life as well).

At the home of many Dutch people, the birthday guests sit in a circle. The drawback to this is that people hardly mingle. Fortunately there are also birthday celebrations where the guests walk around and talk to each other in small groups. While at the same time the host or hostess goes around the room serving, for instance, hors d'oeuvres and drinks. Sometimes there is also a buffet with delicious things to nibble as well as drinks and then you can just help yourself.

When a Dutch person turns fifty, they celebrate a special birthday, because as the Dutch say, he or she has seen Abraham (a man) or Sarah (a woman). Some people even place a doll dressed as Abraham or Sarah in front of their home so that everybody knows that he or she is now fifty. Especially outside big cities, the neighbours and family decorate the house of the person who is having their birthday. There are also special Abraham and Sarah *speculaaspoppen* (large decorated gingerman-and-woman cookies) that make marvellous presents. This custom is supposedly related to a Bible text from John 8:57: 'Thou art not yet fifty years old, and hast thou seen Abraham?' This suggests that someone who turns fifty will meet Abraham. The names Abraham and Sarah refer to the Biblical couple, of the same names, who gave birth to their son late in life. It is not known when the custom of Abraham and Sarah dolls began in the Netherlands. But it apparently became very popular in the 1950s. *Speculaaspoppen* such as these were even used as decoration for the fiftieth birthday celebration of Queen Juliana in 1959 as well as that of her husband Prince Bernhard in 1961.

The Dutch are also fond of celebrating wedding anniversaries: twenty-five years (silver) and fifty years (golden) are the most important.

Children

Visiting a Dutch person at home might very well include visiting that person's (small) children: they will be walking in and out, watching television or playing on the computer in the same room. Dutch children differ from children elsewhere. To begin with, they are strikingly independent. They frequently bicycle to school by themselves, play outside on the street and often arrange their own play-dates with friends. This is of course much easier than in other countries, because the Dutch tend to live somewhat 'on top of each other' in rows of modest (attached) houses with small back-yards.

The children are also strikingly assertive, as one Dutch saying goes: *ze zijn niet op hun mondje gevallen*, meaning they are articulate. Not all foreigners are charmed by this trait; many find Dutch children badly-raised and rude: 'Parents here are too accommodating when it comes to their children. A single rule seems to apply... the one of almost unlimited indulgence.'

Another foreigner added: 'Parents here can't say no to their children. They therefore learn nothing about boundaries and get their own way with almost everything.' The Estonian conductor, Neeme Järvi, of the *Residentie Orkest* of The Hague, misses discipline in particular: 'Surely young people should be told what to do now and then.'

Long ago, foreigners were also surprised by the doting of Dutch parents, which they found excessive. '*Oh, ces enfants gras et joufflus* (Oh those chubby and round-faced children), how much they are loved and even more so, how much they are spoiled,' said a Frenchman in the 18th century. Especially the lack of respect, the impoliteness of these children was – and still is – shocking to foreigners.

The impact of this kind of leniency does not go unnoticed. Due to the fact that children come first in many Dutch households, they may repeatedly interrupt your conversation with their demand for attention. Many expats find this annoying. In public places, such as restaurants and theatres, expats also find themselves irritated by noisy children who are left to run wild. Parents don't intervene and even look on grinning. 'As long as our kids are having fun!' is the way they see it. Many Dutch poems, such as the two (translated) excerpts that follow, attest to just how much Dutch children are indulged:

Children
Jan Pieter Heije (1867)
(Translation: Lorraine T. Miller)

...Oh, that pushing and that pulling,
Oh, that coercion of body and soul...
All that cajoling, all that fear,
All that obedience is killing:
better for children to be children
if they're ever to grow up, my dear!...

Nice and Naughty
Annie M.G. Schmidt (1955)
(Translation: David Colmer)

...I'll do everything that's wrong,
the whole day long, the whole day long!
I want to jump on the settee
and cover it with grime...
I want to scream hysterically,
and take the dog to bed with me...

Dogs and other pets
During your visit to a Dutch person's home, there is a more than average chance that you will trip over the family's dog or cat. The Dutch are crazy about animals. More than half of the households in the Netherlands have one. Just take a look at this list:

- aquarium fish   2.9 million
- pond fish   2 million
- dogs   1.8 million
- cats   3.4 million
- rabbits   0.6 million
- rodents   0.4 million
- horses and ponies   0.3 million
- reptiles and amphibians   0.1 million
- songbirds and exotic birds   2.6 million
- carrier pigeons   1 million

So you see: more than five million dogs and cats alone!

In the Netherlands, a pet is basically a full-fledged member of the family. If an animal falls ill, people are willing to go to all extremes (and pay thousands of euros) to make this cherished family member better again. An MRI-scan for Whiskers, chemotherapy for Spot or surgery to insert a pin in Tweety's broken foot – it is all just routine for specialised *dierenartsen* (veterinary surgeons).

This love the Dutch express for their pets often goes beyond the grave: in death notices in the newspaper, listed among the surviving members of the family (spouse, children, parents), you may see the name of a dog or cat – sometimes even accompanied by a paw print or a tagline such as 'with a lick from Hector'.

There are also loads of dogs on the street, on the beach, in parks and woodlands to the amazement (and irritation) of many expats. 'Dogs are sniffing all over the place in the Netherlands!' a

Russian exclaimed with a dirty look. And another: 'I hate that there is dog poop everywhere.' Other expats pointed out that there are also people who object to dogs for religious reasons – for instance Muslims.

However, the Dutch do not always care what others think about their love of animals, as illustrated by this true story:

A man is walking on the beach. A woman with dog approaches him. The dog leaps against the man and licks his face. The woman calls out: 'He's harmless! He's harmless!' Then the man falls to his hands and knees, leaps against the woman and licks her face, at the same time exclaiming: 'I'm harmless! I'm harmless!'

Therefore, don't be shocked when you are visiting Dutch people at home and a dog or a cat occupies a prominent place: on the sofa, on the table or against your legs. Or if the cat nestles on your lap and claws your stockings. Oh, you find this objectionable? Then make this clear in a pleasant yet decisive way. If this does not seem to help and your host or hostess does not intervene, best to say you are allergic to the animal in question... And do not feel obliged to elaborate as to whether this is a physical or mental allergy.

The Dutch love affair with dogs is actually not something new, as illustrated by many Dutch paintings since the Golden Age. In these works, dogs are often depicted: on the street or with people at home, in the tavern...yes even in church. It was once very common to take your dog along with you to worship services. But then they had to behave themselves, because if they did not, a special servant of the church called a *hondenslager* (literally dog butcher) removed them from the premises (but he didn't then slaughter them).

Keep in mind that a dog traditionally symbolises loyalty and watchfulness. This is even visible at the tomb of William I of Orange, *Vader des Vaderlands* (Father of the Country) in the *Nieuwe Kerk* (New Church) in Delft. The Prince is carved in white marble, lying on his deathbed, with his faithful dog at his feet.

Do you yourself have a dog? Then better to leave your pet at home if you are going to visit someone. But if your dog must accompany you, first ask your host or hostess if it is all right. And when you are about to receive guests? Then ask if they mind that your pet is around and about the house during their visit.

'Common sense is not always common practice.'
(Sabine Anthony, Leiden University, 2005)

VI

FROM THE CRADLE TO THE GRAVE:

IMPORTANT OCCASIONS

How should you, as a foreigner, respond to so-called *familieberichten* (family notices)? The Dutch generally announce official events such as births, marriages and deaths in the newspaper and/or with a personalised (printed) card. These family notices indicate who has been born, who has died and who has gotten married. So, it is possible that you will come across a notice from a colleague or acquaintance about such an event in the newspaper, or you might be sent such an announcement by mail. What should you do then? This chapter individually examines the formalities related to these kinds of occasions, followed by explanations of two unique Dutch events: the *promotie* (doctorate ritual) and *Sinterklaas* (the Feast of St. Nicholas).

❖❖

Responding to (official) announcements

Announcements published in the newspaper are primarily meant to serve as notification. Therefore, you are not required to respond. But if you would like to, you certainly could. There is nothing against sending a friendly congratulation to new parents or a couple who has recently married, especially when the address is indicated in the newspaper. This applies even more so in the case of a death. The next-of-kin will appreciate all the condolences they receive.

If you personally receive a family (birth, marriage or death) announcement via the post, you are expected to respond, at least in writing. You can also pay a visit, give a present (births, marriages) or react in some other way – this of course all depends on your relationship to the person(s) involved.

In terms of extending Christmas or New Year's wishes: you are not required to respond if the card only contains the name(s) of the sender without a personal message. But if someone has taken the time to write something especially to you on the card, then of course the gracious response is to send a card in return.

✧✧✧

LIFE'S SPECIAL MOMENTS

Birth and baptism

If you receive a birth announcement, the very least you can do is send a written congratulation note. If there is an e-mail address on the card, you may also send congratulations in this modern way. It is also thoughtful to send flowers, a fruit basket or a small present, but this is not required. In any case, do not give a present in advance (imagine if the pregnancy does not go well...) and do not give money as a present either. Of course you can also go on a *kraam-bezoek* (a visit to the parents and new baby). But first make an appointment. The preferred visiting hours and/or resting times of the family are often indicated on the announcement, so respect these. And don't stay too long...after all, having a baby can be a busy time for the young mother (and father).

Many Dutch women choose to give birth at home. Some foreigners find this difficult to comprehend: they equate a home birth with being poor – as if there is not enough money to pay for the hospital. What is also different in the Netherlands, compared to lots of other countries, is that some visitors (neighbours, good friends and of course close family) are already welcome to visit the day following the delivery.

It is also possible that a *kraamdag* is organised, a kind of open house where the newborn is proudly put on display and as many friends and acquaintances as possible visit together. Here you will be offered the traditional Dutch *beschuit-met-muisjes* (see p. 159), coffee or tea and possibly other refreshments.

In terms of a *kraamcadeau* (baby present): as already mentioned, the Dutch have a preference for *gewoon* (normal), so keep it modest. Suitable presents include baby clothes, a (cuddly) toy, a bib or towel embroidered with the infant's name, etc. Only close friends and family should give expensive presents, for instance a traditional silver goblet engraved with the newborn's name. If you don't have a close connection with the new parents, do not arrive with a lavish gift; the Dutch find this embarrassing. This could even lead to misunderstandings, as the following example illustrates: a French expat-couple gave a costly present to a Dutch couple when their first son was born. Some time later the French couple had a child themselves. The Dutch couple's *cadeautje* (small present) was much too modest in the eyes of the French couple. They could not understand and actually got angry, resulting in the end of contact with each other...

Baptism: The christening of a child is a major event in many countries, but in the Netherlands this is celebrated with close family members only.

'Criticizing people, places or anything else, without really knowing them, demonstrates lack of culture, education, and intelligence.'

(Marina Maya Marchioretto, Wageningen University, 2003)

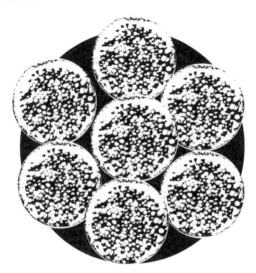

Beschuit-met-muisjes and other Dutch customs

The custom in the Netherlands since the end of the 19th century has been to mark the birth of a baby by eating *beschuit-met-muisjes*, a round toast-like (zwieback) biscuit sprinkled with a smooth candy: pink & white for a girl and blue & white for a boy. These so-called *muisjes* are actually aniseeds coated in sugar, and of course there is a reason for eating these. Anise is apparently very good for a woman's milk production. The name *muisjes* comes from the longer Dutch word *muizenkeutels* (mouse droppings), reminding us of how rapidly mice reproduce. Therefore these *muisjes* symbolise fertility and plenty.

Note: you are supposed to treat your colleagues at work to *be-schuit-met-muisjes*.

For the birth of Princess Catharina-Amalia in 2003, the oldest daughter of Prince Willem-Alexander and his wife Princess Máxima, people throughout the Netherlands were treated to these biscuits sprinkled with *muisjes* but then in bright orange – the colour of the Dutch Royal Family, which traces its lineage back to William of Orange (1533–1584).

Two other practices have gained in popularity in recent years: placing some kind of (paper, wood, even blow-up) stork outside one's home or hanging a row of baby clothes outside on the laundry line to mark the birth of a child. If you happen to see this, do not take it as an open invitation to ring the bell and congratulate the new parents. It is meant more as a festive public announcement.

There is also an old-fashioned Dutch tradition of serving *kandeel* (a liquor called caudle in English) to visitors that come to see the baby. This drink was originally intended for women to regain their strength after the demands of childbirth. The word *kandeel* has its roots in the medieval Latin word *caldellum*, which means a warm drink. *Kandeel* is still available from Dutch wine, beer & spirits merchants (off-licences). Could make a nice baby present?

Engagement

Until around 1970, an engagement in the Netherlands was celebrated with a reception, presents and a festive diner. Nowadays,
engagements are hardly celebrated officially except perhaps by the
Dutch Royal Family.

Marriage

In the Netherlands you may choose to get married once (by a city
official) or twice. The first stage is always the civil ceremony – this
is required by law. Only when this has occurred, may the marriage
be sanctified with a religious ceremony. This can take place all in
one day or on two separate days.

Homohuwelijk (same-sex marriages): Since 2001, it has been
possible in the Netherlands for two men or two women to marry.
The terms and conditions for partners in a homosexual or lesbian
marriage are nearly the same as a marriage between a man and a
woman. In addition, gay couples in the Netherlands can now also
adopt children if they so desire.

Furthermore, the so-called registered partnership has existed
here since 1998. This is another option to establish the legality of a
relationship.

Huwelijksaankondiging (announcement of a forthcoming marriage): Keep in mind that according to Dutch custom, the announcement of a forthcoming marriage is at the same time an invitation. If you receive such a notice it means you are invited to
both the wedding ceremony (civil and/or religious) and the recep-

tion (if any). You can either attend alone, if so desired with your partner, with or without children. You do not have to make this known in advance.

This same custom does not apply in other countries. There an announcement is only that. Those who are invited to the reception receive a separate invitation and are accordingly expected to R.S.V.P. (*répondez, s'il vous plaît*, 'please reply').

However, when it comes to other kinds of wedding celebrations in the Netherlands – for example a *déjeuner-dînatoire* (lunch buffet), a sit-down dinner or a black-tie affair – a separate (printed or handwritten) invitation is sent exclusively to the people invited. In that case, you are expected to R.S.V.P. to say if you are planning to come.

Cadeaus (presents): In the Netherlands, you are not expected to give the bridal pair hundreds of euros as is the custom in a number of other countries. A modest present or something on their wish list is sufficient. Information about what kinds of gifts the bridal couple might want is usually supplied in a separate letter sent around by the witnesses or best man.

You can sometimes consult a bridal wishlist in a specific shop or access it via a website and order a present online – something not too expensive (if you are a poor student) or something costly (if you are a family member or a dear friend). Sometimes, a group gift is organised. Then you only have to contribute a certain amount of money. In these cases, your present (with your name mentioned or visiting card attached) will simply be delivered directly to the bridal couple by the shop, by the witnesses, or by the website from which it was ordered.

It is best not to give your present on the actual day of the wedding, for practical reasons: a wedding day is hectic, especially for the bridal couple. This means they do not have time to devote to presents that are brought along. At a busy reception, accepting and unpacking gifts can lead to guests having to wait forever in the receiving line.

Some wedding announcements include the image of an envelop with the text *cadeautip* (gift tip). This means the bridal pair would prefer 'cold hard cash'. This is actually a strange state of affairs: a marriage is not a business transaction for which a kind of entry fee is paid in exchange for hospitality. Money should be used to pay for goods and services, not to express bonds of friendship or to demonstrate affection. Apart from this – and as already mentioned – contributing money to purchasing a group present is a different matter.

Clothing: The letter sent around by the witnesses or best man usually contains information about the dress code, for instance: men in morning coats (cutaways), women preferably wearing hats, everybody with a white rose, etc. If there is no information, it's a good idea to ask for clarification.

Songs: A typical Dutch tradition is for family and (university) friends to perform during the wedding reception, dinner or party. Meaning they sing songs or perform comic skits that have been written especially for and about the bridal couple. So do not be surprised if you have to queue up (waiting and waiting to offer your congratulations) because out-of-the-blue a group of guests – conceivably in silly getups – rowdily pushes in front of you, positions themselves opposite the happy couple and begins to sing all kinds of ludicrous songs. Nobody understands what they are singing about except the newlyweds themselves. But no matter: everybody is enjoying themselves and it is just one of those quirky Dutch things that custom dictates.

Death

Someone's death might be announced in the newspaper as well as by regular post. A notice in the newspaper with the Dutch phrase *Enige en algemene kennisgeving* indicates that no further notice will arrive by mail.

Are you a friend of the deceased and/or surviving relatives? In that case, a written condolence (preferably by hand) is fitting. Such a condolence – depending on your relationship with the deceased – could be very brief or more elaborate if you desire. In the latter case you might choose to reminisce a bit, or to reflect on some of the deceased person's memorable qualities.

Not done: Do not send a ready-made expression of condolences in which you only sign your name. Certainly this is easy, but also rather impersonal and it might be interpreted as lacking in true concern – as if it is another thing you have gotten out of the way...this is unkind and therefore impolite. It is also a reason to avoid sending condolences by e-mail. Finally: do not ring the next of kin, unless you know them intimately.

Sometimes there is an opportunity to bid farewell to someone prior to the funeral. It is also possible that the person who has died will be laid out at home. Then you can say goodbye in his or her personal surroundings. During such a (short) visit the deceased is the centre of attention. Pay your respects with a moment of silence by the body and then offer your condolences to the next of kin. After the simple exchange of a few words, it is time for you to leave. Flowers brought along with attached cards can be placed on the coffin stand. Respect the visiting hours (usually stated in the announcement).

Of course, personally being present at the burial or cremation is still the best way of expressing your sympathy. You are not expected to announce your attendance in advance. Appearing in black or dark clothing is preferable, unless a specific dress code is mentioned; in any case be appropriately dressed. Foreigners like the Dutch habit of preparing speeches and telling something about the deceased. They see it as a dignified way of bidding farewell to someone.

At a reception before or after a burial or cremation, first express your condolences to the immediate family such as the deceased person's partner, children, and parents. You should keep it as brief as possible and not begin a drawn out conversation.

PROMOTIE – THE DUTCH DOCTORATE RITUAL

In the Netherlands, when someone receives a doctorate (DPhil, PhD), a unique ceremony called a *promotie* takes place. This traditional and engaging ritual consists of three parts: the public defence of the dissertation (thesis), deliberation by the Opposition Committee, and the bestowing of the title *doctor*. These ceremonies are public – you may attend if you so choose. Several of these ceremonies take place each week at universities around the country. Some are even held in English.

Background

Before looking at the current ritual, let me first say something about the origin of the doctor's degree and the graduation ceremony. Our European university tradition dates back to medieval times when the university of Bologna gave birth to the doctorate. The title of *doctor* was conferred (in law – 'doctor legum' in Latin) at Bologna before 1219. At that time, the doctorate was a qualification which permitted a scholar to become a member of a guild. To obtain this right, the candidate had to take a public examination, which led to the award of the degree of doctor. It was a ceremonial examination, one that the candidate could not fail. This was conducted with great pomp and circumstance, as the doctor's title was prestigious. For centuries, the ceremony basically remained the same all over Europe, with some variations, until the end of the Ancien Régime, around 1800.

However, in the Dutch Republic things unfolded differently. Already in the 17th century Dutch students perceived the doctorate ritual as pompous, showy and ostentatious. Moreover, the cost to them was exorbitant. That is why a cheaper and simpler version was devised: the private *promotie* in a small group, without any hoo ha. This form of the doctorate ritual proved to be highly attractive. From that moment on, Dutch students rarely wanted the traditional ritual. Almost all of them preferred the new, modern form.

Meanwhile, in other European countries the traditional ceremony remained in use. Only during and after the French Revolution were these rituals modernised. In some universities, the lavish public ceremony was simplified, while at others it was abolished altogether. As a result, at many universities the examination was left over as the only doctorate ritual.

Since the Dutch had modernised their ritual much earlier, they only adapted it in the 19th century. That is why the Dutch *promotie* has a unique form, which preserves historical elements, for example the paranymphs and propositions, that disappeared elsewhere. Paradoxically, while we were ahead of the time in the 17th century, now, in the 21st century, our ritual is very traditional and therefore, to Dutch and foreigners alike, rather gratifying.

Characteristic of the ritual

Propositions: Included in the Dutch dissertation system is the tradition of writing a PhD thesis, which is accompanied by a number of *stellingen* (propositions). These propositions (nowadays no longer obligatory at all Dutch universities) must be 'defendable' and some have to be directly related to the thesis itself. Additional propositions provide an indication of the breadth and depth of a candidate's knowledge. While the dissertation itself is usually very specialised, the candidate is expected to display interest and fluency in a broad area of expertise. The 'final proposition' may be more playful, social or politically-oriented and is traditionally therefore a surprise. Final propositions such as these are often printed in Dutch newspapers and there are even small anthologies published; you will find some of them scattered in this book.

Paranymphs: The *promovendus* (doctorand) has to choose two people to act as his or her assistants before and during the graduation process. The paranymphs can be selected from among family members, good friends, fellow students or work colleagues. During the ceremony they stand on either side of the candidate. Their task is to help the candidate: they oblige by pouring water, checking the microphone, arranging papers and of course by offering moral support to the often extremely nervous *promovendus*. Besides these fixed tasks, paranymphs also fulfil the master of ceremony role for any related festivities (reception, dinner, organising a gift). They can be compared to the witnesses at a wedding. The word paranymph has its roots here as well, because the ancient meaning (Greek: *para* = beside, next to; *numphè* = bride, *numphios* = bridegroom) is page.

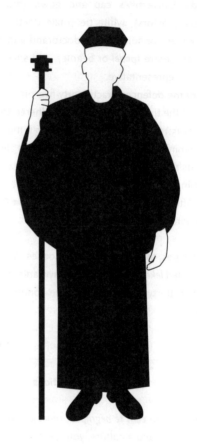

Hora est!

Dress code: University's cap and gown (professors), dark (woman's) suit (doctors), white tie (male doctorand and paranymphs), dark dress or suit (female doctorand and paranymphs), black gown and sceptre (*pedel* or beadle), and silver chain for the rector or his/her representative.

Duration of the defence: Exactly forty-five minutes. It's important to note that the times announced are adhered to strictly. If the invitation states 15:15 as the starting time, then it means exactly 3.15 p.m. and not a minute later. Afterwards, nobody is allowed to enter. The beadle ends the defence by striking his sceptre on the floor and loudly exclaiming (in Latin): *Hora est!* (It is time!, i.e. to stop the disputation). After deliberation by the Opposition Committee the doctorate is awarded.

At some universities, the promovendus chooses to or is required to first give a so-called *lekenpraatje* (literally layman's talk): a presentation of fifteen to thirty minutes about the contents of his or her doctoral thesis.

Academic propositions

Om een cultuur echt te begrijpen, moet je haar taal leren.
'To truly understand a culture, you must learn its language.'
(Christina Michler, Technical University Delft, 2005)

'As famous food-lovers, French people
always need their survival kit in Holland.'
(Muriel Derrien, Wageningen University, 2007)

Werkende mannen die niet zorgen,
zorgen ervoor dat vrouwen niet werken.
'Working men, who don't contribute at home,
contribute to women not working.'
(B. Dauwe, University of Groningen, 1999)

SINTERKLAAS, 'FEAST OF ST. NICHOLAS'

Sinterklaas, the Dutch Feast of St. Nicholas, celebrated yearly on 5 December, is by far the most popular Dutch holiday: it is number one of the top hundred Dutch traditions. In his red robe and mitre, toting a bishop's staff, with long white beard, on top of his white horse and accompanied by his helper *Zwarte Piet* (Black Pete), the figure of *Sinterklaas* is nothing less than remarkable. Year in and year out, in mid-November, he makes his grand entrance by steamboat and is festively welcomed, all of this broadcasted live on television.

Reporters from the German TV station ZDF, whom I accompanied while they were shooting an item about this in 2007, could not believe their eyes...The crowds! The enthusiasm! Never before had they experienced a national holiday like this one. The *Zwarte Pieten* were tossing traditional Dutch sweets elsewhere unknown: *peper-noten*, *speculaas*, *kikkers* and *muizen* (see p. 143). *Sinterklaas* mounted his horse and proceeded triumphantly along the crowds, as thousands sung their throats sore with special St. Nicholas songs.

Starting from the day he arrives in the Netherlands, children may set out a shoe at night to be filled with sweets. Then St. Nicholas on his horse clatters over the rooftops with his Petes tossing small presents through the chimneys. For the popular *pakjesavond* (family present evening on 5 December), the Dutch make *surprises* (funny packages) and *gedichten* (poems) to mildly mock, praise or encourage someone else.

Sinterklaas was originally a Catholic saint: St. Nicholas (circa 280 – circa 342). He was once the Bishop of Myra (now Demre in Turkey). Long after his death, in the 11th century, his relics were taken to Bari in Italy, to protect them against the advancing Turks. Thanks to all kinds of wonderous stories, Nicolas became a much-revered saint throughout Europe. He was not only the patron saint of sailors (allegedly he saved those who were shipwrecked) but also the patron saint of children and the poor (because of his great love for his fellow man and his generosity). The evening of 5 December, which proceeds the day on which he died (a Saint's day used to be celebrated the evening before), was commemorated more and more in the Netherlands. In Dordrecht, as early as 1360, children were free the entire day and received money from the municipal treasury. In 1427, poor children placed their footwear in the St. Nicholas Church in Utrecht. Rich people then filled this.

But then the Reformation came: celebrating *Sinterklaas* was seen as a Catholic superstition by Calvinists and they were against it. So this festivity went from being a public religious holiday to being celebrated in the privacy of one's own home. A famous painting from 1665 by Jan Steen depicts how the holiday was observed at that time: as presents fall through the chimney, St. Nicholas songs are sung. *Sinterklaas* also took on a function related to upbringing: he rewarded good children and punished those who were bad.

Sinterklaas versus Santa Claus

The name Santa Claus is an American-accented version of the Dutch name *Sinterklaas*. Many people don't realise it, but he is actually one in the same person. Though it is not exactly known when the idea of this figure was first brought from Northern Europe to New Amsterdam – now Manhattan – it is probably safe to say he came with the early Dutch settlers. Later, in the 1820s, he began to acquire his recognisable trappings: reindeer, sleigh, bells.

Via the Americans, this *Kerstman* (Father Christmas) or Santa Claus returned to Europe, where he first became popular in Great Britain and later also in Germany and the German-speaking areas of Central Europe. In the Netherlands, in the 1990s, there was something of a battle between our time-honoured *Sinterklaas* and the jolly ho-ho-ho exclaiming Santa Claus. There was talk of the dangers of the encroaching American *Kerstman,* who threatened to elbow out the traditional Dutch celebration. The blame was attributed to large commercial companies which inundated shops as early as October with Father Christmases, in an attempt to seduce the Dutch into already shopping for Christmas. The very existence of our own *Sinterklaas* celebration was at risk! Action groups were even established. Fortunately, *Sinterklaas* won out. As mentioned earlier, in a survey about the most important traditions in the Netherlands, conducted in 2008, he received by far the most votes.

❀❀

What does *Sinterklaas* have to do with good manners?
When it comes down to it, *Sinterklaas* is the most respected man in the Netherlands. Everyone addresses him with the polite form of *u* (you) in Dutch, speaks to him in more than one-word sentences: *Ja Sinterklaas, Dank u wel, Sinterklaas* (Yes, *Sinterklaas*, Thank you very much, *Sinterklaas*) and is well-mannered in his presence. The *Goedheiligman* (Good, holy man) stimulates this ideal behaviour. He always has a large book with him, too, in which he jots down the good and bad deeds of children (and sometimes adults as well). He reprimands them about their naughtiness and rewards them for being good.

Adults also get involved in the festivities: they make so-called *surprises* (funny packages) for family or friends or even their work colleagues and write accompanying poems. These so-called *surprises* are usually arts & crafts projects (they don't have to be museum pieces; it's about having fun), which are somehow related to the person on the receiving end. For instance: a cardboard violin for a friend who has just started taking violin lessons; a paper angel for a colleague who always goes out of his or her way to help others; a giant paper maché mouth for a brother who always needs to have the last word. In the corresponding poems, the present-giver offers commentary about the receiver: praising, complaining, admiring, insulting or just telling the plain truth about them. Naturally, all of this occurs in an upbeat tone because celebrating *Sinterklaas* is meant to be an enjoyable social event. For many people, *Pakjesavond* is the jolliest evening of the Dutch year.

What is also appealing about this holiday is that people have to think about others – about what is going on in another person's life. And as we know, having good manners is also about being able to put yourself in someone else's shoes.

✧✧

La monarchie néerlandaise est moins monarchique
que la République française.
'The Dutch monarchy is not nearly as royal
as the French republic.'
(N. Manson, Leiden University, 2007)

VII

PROTOCOL AND THE DUTCH ROYAL HOUSE

HELP! I'M GOING TO MEET THE QUEEN!

Panic! This might be the first thing that crosses your mind if you are invited to a gathering with Queen Beatrix or other members of the Royal Family. Questions that might come to mind next could include what you should say and how you should dress. Fortunately, you do not need to feel unsure of yourself. Meeting a member of the Royal House is always strictly choreographed, and that is a relief to say the least. You will be guided every step of the way, so that (almost) nothing can go wrong.

Generally speaking, many of the conventions that apply to meeting ordinary people in everyday life apply to meeting members of the Royal Family. However, there are some specific rules, because Queen Beatrix of the Netherlands is the highest-ranking person in society (and members of the Royal House are rather high-ranking as well). So here are some things to take into account:

- ❖ **Be punctual:** At a formal reception, in the presence of one or more members of the Royal Family, one should always arrive before them and leave after them. Note: punctuality applies to departing too. It is a sign of respect.

❖ **Rise:** At the arrival and departure of the queen or other royalty you are expected to stand up and turn towards them. Depending on the occasion, this goes hand-in-hand with something ceremonial. A court dignitary will loudly exclaim *Hare Majesteit de Koningin!* (Her Majesty the Queen!), followed by everybody in the room rising. In a fitting silence, the queen (the Prince of Orange, Princess Máxima, etc.) will then enter followed by a *hofdame* (lady-in-waiting), equerry, possibly other members of her royal household and possibly one or more officials directly involved with the events of that day. The people in the room may only sit down again once the queen has taken her seat.

❖ **Introductions:** As a rule, you may only be introduced to someone of royalty by a member of the retinue. Therefore, do not take it upon yourself to approach the queen (the Prince of Orange, Princess Máxima...) to introduce yourself or to strike up a conversation. This rule is there to protect them. After all, there is a good chance that many people present will want to talk to them. If the queen wants to meet you, for instance, then a member of the retinue (lady-in-waiting, equerry) will approach you and make the introduction. The courtiers pay careful attention to who speaks to the queen, when and for how long. They intervene if necessary and replace one conversation partner with another, so that the company changes and the queen can speak to all the people she wants to meet. If it is a small gathering (a dinner or modest reception at the palace) those invited are requested to send a brief curriculum vitae in advance to Her Majesty's secretariat. The queen reads these carefully in advance, in order to have an idea about her invited guests. Instead of having to ask questions such as 'What kind of work do you do?' or 'Where do you come from?' she can immediately begin a conversation with you about what is of interest to her. This usually leads to meaningful and lively discussions.

- ❖ **Curtsy** (to the queen or other members of the Royal House): This is a formal sign of respect or admiration from a woman, done by bending the knees with one foot in front of the other while lowering the body. This practice is no longer required in the Netherlands because Queen Juliana did away with it in 1953. However curtsying is still customary in other monarchies, such as Great Britain, Denmark and Spain.
- ❖ **Terms of address:** Queen Beatrix is addressed in Dutch as *majesteit* and/or *mevrouw* (Your Majesty and/or Ma'am); both Prince Willem-Alexander and Princess Máxima are addressed as *koninklijke hoogheid* (Your Royal Highness).
- ❖ **Behaviour:** One is still expected to act in a reserved way in the presence of the queen or a member of the Royal Family. This is not as stiff as it used to be, but a certain distance is still required. This ensures a degree of dignity.
- ❖ **Official audience:** At an official audience, the queen (or another member of the Royal House) speaks first and also indicates when that audience has come to an end.

- **Leaving:** As a rule, the honoured or most important person is the first to leave – this means: only once he or she has departed the others are free to go.
- **Clothing:** The dress code for visiting the Dutch queen or a member of the Royal House is usually stated in the invitation.
- **No gifts:** It is unusual to bring flowers or another gift if one is received at Court (unless you are close friends with someone in the Royal Family).
- **Tipping:** Never tip at the Royal Court.
- Always stand facing someone of royalty; do not turn your back on them.
- It is considered impolite on the way to the tribune, podium, etc. to walk in front of the queen, because one should never obstruct her view. Therefore remember to pass behind her on your way to wherever you might need to go.
- **No empty seat:** If someone stands up from the chair beside the queen (for example to give a speech), then the person sitting closest to her is expected to (temporarily) sit there instead; no empty seats beside the queen!
- **Staircase:** One has to ascend a staircase in front of the queen and descend a staircase following behind her.

❖❖

What are the advantages of protocol?
Protocol is a valuable tool. It ensures that everybody – including

you – knows exactly what they should do: What is the dress code? Who sits where? Who speaks when and for how long with the queen?, etc. It guarantees that everything goes like clockwork. Consequently, Queen Beatrix carefully adheres to it. Thanks to protocol, official audiences and gatherings happen smoothly and in a dignified, calm and purposeful way. Protocol has existed since the congress of Vienna in 1815; it was then decided to create official ways of behaving for states as well as important officials and their representatives. Just like with etiquette, these ways of behaving are based on two familiar principles: take others into consideration and be clear. In essence, etiquette provides the rules of behaviour between people, whereas protocol concerns the conduct of states towards one another. One could say, that these paradigms illustrate the micro and macro of relations, both at a personal and international level.

Beatrix' mother, Queen Juliana (1909–2004), did not like protocol: she preferred things to be *gewoon* (normal). But this often caused difficulties for others. She was anything but normal; she was our head of state. So when she was visiting somewhere and said: 'Stop that silly nonsense! Just pretend I am not here...' then everybody got confused. Should Queen Juliana sit in the first row or not? Did someone have to escort her inside or should she be left to do as she so desires? Should someone take her coat, or will she take care of this herself? The queen, who longed to be normal, threw everybody into a tizzy. Queen

Beatrix witnessed the problems associated with this and that is why she does it differently.

The steadfastness of protocol has another advantage. If the Netherlands does not want to do something, then they can simply say that it is according to protocol or that protocol does not permit it. This makes protesting or insisting pointless. The president of Slovakia related how he had hoped the Dutch queen would visit the High Tatra Mountains in his country during a state visit in 2007. Unfortunately, this did not happen. Why not? 'Oh', the president replied: '...dictated by Dutch protocol.' He then continued with a riddle: 'Do you know the difference between protocol and a terrorist? Answer: you can negotiate with a terrorist, but with your protocol, no way!'

❖❖

STATE VISITS

Just like other heads of state, Queen Beatrix regularly goes on so-called state visits. Visits such as these have not existed all that long. It is said that the French emperor Napoleon III was the originator. He came up with this idea of the state visit and it turned out to be a successful diplomatic tool when he needed the support of Queen Victoria of England in 1855. Her visit, with its official touch of prestige and much pomp and splendour, ended up being very useful for doing (state) business. Until then, heads of state – almost all of them monarchs and related to each other in one way or another – had limited themselves to reciprocal royal family visits.

Several foreign powers followed Napoleon's example. In 1883, the Dutch king Willem III invited the Belgian king Leopold II to visit: it became the first official state visit to the Netherlands. Large, enthusiastic crowds filled the streets of Amsterdam.

The practice when receiving state visitors: The queen goes to the airport or train station to welcome her guest. The visit mainly happens in Amsterdam, and the visiting head of state stays in the Royal Palace on Dam Square. There the traditional laying of a wreath takes place at the War Memorial and a state banquet is held in the palace. Around two hundred guests attend such a dinner.

A head of state might also come on an official working visit. Then he or she is not personally welcomed by the queen and stays at the Noordeinde Palace in The Hague where the queen also works. The programme then primarily takes place in The Hague and sometimes also elsewhere in the country. There is less pomp and circumstance related to such a visit.

During state visits, presents are traditionally exchanged. These are meant as mementos and therefore, according to the experts, not supposed to be too expensive. Moreover, such a gift is a means to promote one's own country. Artistic as the queen herself is, she has a preference for giving works by modern Dutch artists that she has personally selected.

Titles held by Queen Beatrix

Queen Beatrix signs official documents as: *Wij Beatrix, bij de gratie Gods, Koningin der Nederlanden, Prinses van Oranje-Nassau, etc., etc., etc....* (We Beatrix, by the grace of God, Queen of the Netherlands, Princess of Orange-Nassau, etc., etc, etc...) It is perhaps interesting to note that the Dutch dynasty traces itself back to a French prince's title (Orange) and a German count's title (Nassau).

Repeating the etc. three times above refers to the title Princess of Lippe-Biesterfeld (the family name of Beatrix' father Prince Bernhard) and is also a reminder of the many titles the Princes of Orange-Nassau held until 1815: all of these were connected to places in the Netherlands, Belgium, Luxembourg, Germany and France. These (dormant) titles are: Marquis of Veere and Vlissingen; Earl of Katzenelnbogen, Vianden, Diez, Spiegelberg, Buren, Leerdam and Culemborg; Viscount of Antwerp; Baron of Breda, Diest, Beilstein, the city of Grave, the land of Cuyk, IJsselstein, Cranendonk, Eindhoven, Liesveld, Herstel, Warneton, Arlay and Nozeroy; Baron of Ameland; Lord of Borculo, Bredevoort, Lichtenvoorde, het Loo, Geertruidenberg, Clundert, Zevenbergen, Hoge and Lage Zwaluwe, Naaldwijk, Polanen, Sint-Maartensdijk, Soest, Baarn, Ter Eem, Willemstad, Steenbergen, Montfoort, Sankt Vith, Bütgenbach, Daasburg, Niervaart, Turnhout and Besançon.

Lettres de Créance – Credentials

On Wednesdays, you might notice coaches riding through the streets of The Hague, accompanied by footman and a few riders in fine uniforms. A new ambassador from abroad is on his or her way to Noordeinde Palace to present his or her credentials to Queen Beatrix. This official act usually takes place with much ceremony and therefore according to an array of rules determined by protocol: an escort, military tribute, etc. The new ambassador is taken by carriage from his or her residence or chancellery. He or she is accompanied by a chamberlain of the queen, the director of protocol or the secretary-general of the Ministry of Foreign Affairs. The dress code specifies a morning coat, ambassador's uniform or that country's national costume. Arriving at Palace Noordeinde, the national anthem of that ambassador's country is played. Then the ambassador walks a red carpet while inspecting the Dutch guard of honour.

This inspection harks back to historical times, when monarchs visited each other and displayed their armed power as a sign of security and protection. With weapons displayed, all the soldiers stood neatly ranked in rows and the visiting sovereign strode past to inspect them. 'Take a good look, they will not hurt you, you are safe' was the message conveyed. The present-day inspection of the guard of honour, also customary during state visits, has survived from this and is now nothing more than a striking formality.

Then the ambassador with his or her entourage enters the palace, greets Her Majesty and hands over his or her credentials to the queen. This is followed by a conversation between the queen and the ambassador that is generally, as would be expected, about his or her country. The queen eventually gives the sign that the meeting has come to an end.

Prinsjesdag, 'Day of the Queen's Speech'

On the third Tuesday in September, the Dutch queen addresses a joint session of the Upper and Lower Houses of the Parliament (States General) in the *Ridderzaal* (Knights' Hall) on the *Binnenhof* in The Hague. This *troonrede* (address from the throne) describes the main aspects of government policy for the coming parliamentary session. This event is prescribed by the Dutch constitution.

Have you as an expat been invited to attend? Play close attention to the instructions you receive, also concerning the dress code. On this particular day, the women are the centre of attention – primarily because, over the years, *Prinsjesdag* has developed into an annual parading of hats. The media provide extensive coverage of the hats worn by the distinguished ladies who attend. So if you are thinking of wearing a hat, order early, because milliners and hat shops are quite busy at this time of the year.

Procession: At precisely 1 p.m. the queen, accompanied by other members of the Royal Family, leaves Noordeinde Palace for the *Binnenhof* in the *Gouden Koets* (Golden Coach), escorted by court dignitaries and a military guard of honour. An honour guard and military bands are present at Palace Noordeinde as well as waiting at the Dutch parliament building and royal gun salutes are fired at one-minute intervals to inform the people that the head of state is on her way to the joint session of the States General.

Ceremony: Once the queen has arrived, the band strikes up the national anthem. The queen and the other members of the Royal Family salute the flag and ascend the steps to the Knight's Hall. The Speaker announces the queen's arrival, a signal for everybody present to rise. The queen proceeds to the throne, from where she delivers her speech. After the queen's closing words, the Speaker exclaims 'Long live the Queen', which is followed by three cheers from everyone present. That concludes this special joint session of the two Houses; it is a purely ceremonial occasion with no political discussion. The entire royal entourage is escorted to the door and the Speaker declares the session closed. The queen exits the hall and the procession returns to the palace.

The name: *Prinsjesdag* originally marked the birthday celebration of the Princes of Orange. In the 17th and 18th centuries, this day provided an opportunity to demonstrate loyalty to the House of Orange. This probably explains why this name is used since the 19th century for the ceremonial opening of Parliament.

4 EN 5 MEI-HERDENKING, '4 & 5 MAY COMMEMORATION'

Bevrijdingsdag (Liberation Day) is celebrated every year in the Netherlands on 5 May. On this day in 1945, the country was liberated after the capitulation of Germany and Japan. The commemoration of the dead (*Dodenherdenking*) takes place the evening before, on 4 May. People who have perished in wartime situations and peace operations since the outbreak of World War II are commemorated throughout the country. The ceremony has a long tradition: as early as 1946, commemorations took place all over the Netherlands as a tribute to victims of World War II. Since 1956, the National Monument on Dam Square in Amsterdam has been the site of a national commemoration with a placing of wreaths by the queen.

A siren sounds on 4 May, exactly at 8 p.m., to signal that two minutes of silence have commenced. This applies across the Netherlands. Also people who are underway (driving in cars, cyclists, pedestrians, etc.) are expected to stop. Do not disturb the silence!

Why two minutes? One explanation is that in 1919, King George V of Great Britain requested a moment of silence lasting two minutes for the (meanwhile annual) 11 November commemoration of the victims of World War I. Anyway, two minutes is more than one minute. For instance, a minute of complete silence might be observed for an 'ordinary' commemoration of someone's death or during a solemn procession. The 4 May commemoration is a national event, occurs on a larger scale and therefore lasts two minutes. Interesting to note: a three-minute silence was observed at a ceremony held in the Netherlands on 14 September 2001 to commemorate victims of the 9-11 terrorist attack in New York City.

KONINGINNEDAG, 'QUEEN'S DAY'

Queen Beatrix officially celebrates her birthday every year on 30 April: *Koninginnedag*. Her own birthday actually falls on 31 January, but as a tribute to her mother Queen Juliana, who was born on 30 April, she has maintained this spring date for *Koninginnedag*. This day is a national holiday celebrated by all kinds of (street) parties and other events. Lots of people like to dress themselves in orange clothes. Many cities are transformed into a giant flea market and you do not have to worry about paying any taxes on the goods you sell that day. The Dutch save things the entire year and then put it outside on Queen's Day, in hopes of getting rid of all their old stuff.

Queen Beatrix and other members or the Royal Family visit official festivities in one or possibly two different locations each year. These royal visits are always broadcast live on television.

Europa moet één monarchie worden.
'Europe should be a single monarchy.'
(Albert Kamping, University of Groningen, 2000)

SELECT BIBLIOGRAPHY

- *A dictionary of Dutchness; From ATV to ZZP'er.* The Hague 2007 (info: www.DutchNews.nl).
- Amicis, Edmondo de. *Nederland en zijn bewoners.* Utrecht/Antwerp 1985 (original title *Olanda*, 1874).
- Birschel, Annette. *Do ist der Bahnhof. Nederland door Duitse ogen.* Amsterdam 2008.
- Bodt, Saskia de. *Children of Holland.* The Hague 2009.
- *Calvinismus. Die Reformierten in Deutschland und Europa.* (Catalogue Exhibition Deutsches Historisches Museum, Berlin) Dresden 2009.
- Daniëls, Wim. *Talking Dutch* (the story of the origin and development of the Dutch language). Rekkem 2005 (available in four languages: English, Dutch, French, German).
- Ditzhuyzen, Reinildis van. 'The "creatio doctoris": convergence or divergence of ceremonial forms?', in: Tor Halversen, Atle Nyhagen (ed.), *The Bologna Process and the shaping of the future knowledge societies.* Bergen (Norway) 2005, pp. 128–140.
- Dunk, Thomas von der. 'Incognito aber Stadtbekannt: Joseph II. auf Reisen in Holland', in: *Germanie. De Achttiende Eeuw*, Volume 40 (2008), pp. 87–114.
- Erasmus, Desiderius. *Etiquette* (with an introduction by Reinildis van Ditzhuyzen). Amsterdam 2001 (original publication Basel 1530).
- *Expat Survival Guide, The. Your essential guide to living in the Netherlands.* Haarlem 2008 (info: www.expatica.com).
- Favell, Adrian. *Eurostars and Eurocities: free movement and mobility in an integrating Europe.* Malden MA (USA) 2008.

- Horst, Han van der. *The Low Sky. Understanding the Dutch*. Schiedam 2006.

- Jobse-van Putten, Jozien. *Eenvoudig maar voedzaam. Cultuurgeschiedenis van de dagelijkse maaltijd in Nederland*. Nijmegen 1995.

- Kaldenbach, Hans. *Act normal! 99 tips for dealing with the Dutch*. Amsterdam 2006.

- Krol, Ronald van de. *Native English for Nederlanders. A personal, cultural and grammatical guide*. Amsterdam 2008.

- Prosperi, Graciela de Savornin Lohman-. *One foot on either shore, a Dutch-Argentinian Portrait*. The Hague 2003.

- Rosenkranz, Stefanie. 'Kicken, Kiffen, Käse: Holland, unser putziger Nachbar', in: *Stern* 26 (19 June 2008), pp. 52–58.

- Sanders, Ewoud. *Borrelwoordenboek: 750 volksnamen voor onze glazen boterham*. The Hague/Antwerp 1997.

- Schama, Simon. *The embarrassment of riches. An interpretation of Dutch culture in the Golden Age*. New York 1987.

- Schlizio, Boris U., Ute Schürings and Alexander Thomas. *Beruflich in den Niederlanden. Trainingsprogramm für Manager, Fach- und Führungskräfte*. Göttingen 2008.

- Trompenaars, Fons, and Charles Hampden-Turne. *Riding the waves of culture. Understanding cultural diversity in business*. London 2002.

- Vaessen, Ad. *Duitsers onder de Nederlanders*. Houten 2008.

- Vossestein, Jacob. *Dealing with the Dutch*. Amsterdam 2004.

- Vree, Wilbert van. *Nederland als vergaderland. Opkomst en verbreiding van een vergaderregime*. Groningen (diss.) 1994.

- White, Colin, and Laurie Boucke. *The Undutchables. An observation of the Netherlands: its culture and its inhabitants*. Amsterdam 2001⁴.

- Wouters, Cas, *Informalization: manners and emotions since 1890*. Los Angeles 2007.
- Zonneveld, Jacques van, and Chris Nigten. *Europeans in The Hague*. The Hague 1998.

With my sincere thanks to the many expats in the Netherlands who shared their personal experiences with me, as well as the following organisations and individuals:

- *ACCESS*, The Hague (Administrative Committee to Coordinate English-Speaking Services) – Carol Wooley
- Frederike van den Berg-Mijnlieff
- *Bronovo Hospital* – Dr. Henk Berendsen
- Erik Busser
- *Deutsch-Niederländische Handelskammer / DNHK* (German-Dutch Chamber of Commerce) – Dr. Lars Björn Gutheil
- *Église Wallonne* / Wallonian Church, The Hague
- *Expatriate Archive Centre*, The Hague – Judy Moody-Stuart, Elske van Holk
- *Français du Monde / ADFE* (Association of French people overseas), Dutch branch – Catherine Libeaut
- *Genootschap Nederland Duitsland* (Dutch-German Association) – Dorothee von Flemming
- *Hora est*, www.hora-est.nl (Dutch and English propositions accompanying PhD theses presented at universities in the Netherlands) – Paul ten Hove
- *Outpost*, The Hague, Royal Dutch Shell – Karen Goodman
- Maxine Sutton
- *Taleninstituut Regina Coeli* – Nickey Eadie, Martin Howard, Vincent McGourty, Veronica Timmer
- *THIS* (The Hague International Spirit) – Nicole van Haelst & Dr. Gary Hays

Index